Using Environmental Archaeology

Myra Shackley

B T BATSFORD LTD LONDON

British Library cataloguing in publication data
Shackley, Myra
 Using environmental archaeology.
  1. Society, Primitive
  I. Title
  306   GN478
  ISBN 0-7134-4849-1

ISBN 0 7134 4849 1 (cased)
ISBN 0 7134 4850 4 (limp)

Typeset by Servis Filmsetting Ltd
and printed in Great Britain by
Anchor-Brendon Ltd, Tiptree, Essex

for the publishers
B.T. Batsford Ltd
4 Fitzhardinge Street
London W1H 0AH

Contents

Acknowledgements

I am greatly indebted to all my friends, colleagues and students who have contributed to this book by way of advice, ideas and the provision of obscure examples. Figs. 1–2, 5, 7, 21, 30, 37, 41–2, 49, 55, 63–4 and 67 are the work of Lorna Smith, and figs. 4, 6, 8–9, 18, 23, 28, 31–3, 36, 38–40, 43, 48, 56, 58, 61, 66, 68–9 will be immediately recognisable as reconstruction drawings produced by the inimitable Andy Clark.

The following individuals and organisations have kindly provided permission to reproduce illustrations; fig. 20 (Prof. B.W. Cunliffe), fig. 29 (Prof. A.C. Blanc), fig. 34 (Prof. W. Muller-Christensen), fig. 35 (Tony Gouldwell), figs. 44–5 (Leicester Museum), fig. 47 (David Neal), figs. 52–3 (Viking Ship Museum, Copenhagen), figs. 51–4 (Dept. of Urban Archaeology, London), fig. 57 (Charlotte Roberts), fig. 59 (Prof. F. Fischer), fig. 65 (Dierdre O'Sullivan). Unless otherwise stated, the photographs are my own.

Illustrations

Preface

In this book I have attempted to reconstruct, from their organic remains, something about different aspects of the lives of early people, concentrating on results actually obtained rather than hypotheses still dreamed-of. The result is a low-level synthesis, rather than an in-depth account of methodology. There is little talk of conceptual frameworks, cognitive forms of reference and current advances in the development of paradigmatic models which may then be applied to archaeological data. This is not a reflection of any deep disapproval on the author's part of all the significant advances made in archaeological method and theory in the last 20 years. Quite simply, an introduction to the practical use of environmental archaeology is not the place for such discussion.

The first archaeologists were concerned with the shape of evidence: the form of a pot, the structure of a building. Over the years immense technical advances in both the field and the laboratory have combined to generate different sets of questions – we might now be equally concerned, for example, about what the pot had originally contained, how it was made, what function it performed. With every passing year the volume of archaeological data expands well beyond the capacity of any one individual to analyse and understand it and, moreover, we have realised that we know little of the concepts which underly the data, hence the constant search for structures to put the evidence that we have into perspective, and so raise questions about the ways in which early people lived. The search for structure is far from over but advances in archaeological theory have sometimes been made at the expense of archaeological practice. Sometimes we have been blinded by the brilliance of our own techniques and been reluctant to ask the question 'so what?' when confronted with yet another interminable list of data. This problem is most acutely felt in archaeological science, where, with each passing year, we discover that yet another scientific discipline can help us to interpret the archaeological record better, resulting in the construction of another compound noun and a spate of papers on archaeoethnobotany, palaeoethnoparasitology, etc.

This is a healthy tendency as it shows that archaeology is alive and well and looking for a structure. The problem is that we now have two types of archaeologists; those who approve of 'the quest', and agree that archaeology must be deemed a science, and those who insist that not only is the proper

9

study of mankind still man but that the archaeological scientists are actually deflecting attention away from 'proper' archaeology. They see such 'proper' archaeology as the stitching together of information obtained from artefacts and the excavation of structures, within a neat framework (preferably documentary) so that no unnecessary complications (like additional information about how early agriculture or technology functioned by setting up modern experiments) need obtrude. This is an extreme view and maligns many good archaeologists who will doubtless never speak to me again. However, despite the predictions of many archaeological scientists (including myself) that the last ten years would see a gradual merging of these Two Cultures into something approaching a Compleat Archaeologist, this has not happened, and I sometimes think that the two are further apart than ever.

The squeeze on resources has affected everything in archaeology from sitework to publication, and one of its most insidious results is that progress in integration has been compartmentalised; the botanists who work with archaeological material make progress, the excavators of the sites make progress, but there is seldom any integration of the two, as can be seen by a cursory examination of any series of site reports. How can this situation be remedied? If there is any question of conflict of interest in archaeology it is generally in the work carried out by 'specialists' which is sacrificed, since it is often expensive. The specialist concerned may be busy and his report may not be forthcoming as quickly as the archaeologist requires. Another problem is that a surprising number of non-technical archaeologists require a great deal of convincing that the results of scientific analysis of some of their material can actually contribute a great deal of value to the site. What can it tell them that they don't know already? This is especially true of 'bioarchaeology' – the study of the organic remains left by earlier human communities. When carried out properly, this requires carefully controlled sampling programmes as a prelude to detailed laboratory analysis, which must be accounted for in pre-excavation processing. Only a small proportion of excavators are convinced that it is worthwhile; and how is one to convert the doubters when comparatively little has been published?

One approach, taken in this book, is to start the conversion right at the bottom and look, in a very general way, at the kind of information which has been obtained and what it can tell us about how early communities lived and died. Obviously, there is going to be enough information (of very variable quality) to write an encyclopaedia, so the selection of good examples which make specific points has been necessary. Moreover, since the book is written for people to whom the topic is completely new, it is important to keep it as non-technical as possible. Even so, the reader will find that accounts of the methods used, or the limitations of a particular technique, have crept in (deliberately) and that, by the end, they will have obtained a reasonable overview of what sources we can use to reconstruct different aspects of daily life in antiquity, having gone through a wide variety of cultures, periods and places. This method runs the risk of fragmenting the data too much, and forcing the reader to make great leaps in time. This is why a series of topics has been chosen which provides possibly the greatest insights into the way in which people lived; how, for example, does the archaeologist know about the earliest agriculture, when (and what) the first men hunted or what archaeological evidence there is for drug-taking in antiquity? How can we tell what life was like in a medieval town from looking at its sewers and how can we identify what caused a man's death simply from an examination of his bones?

I have tried to answer these and many other questions in a way that will provide a good read as well as a source of information. For those who would like to continue with this subject in greater detail there is a bibliography at the back of the book with specific references for each chapter. For those who will deeply disapprove of this seemingly frivolous and structureless approach to the writing of an introductory text in archaeology I recommend detailed reading of 'Perspectives' and 'Predictions'. You probably still won't agree with me but at least you will know what I am trying to do. Nobody, except the reader, approves of syntheses but after all, who on earth are books written for?

I
Perspectives

Every academic study is subject to fashions; changes of emphasis dictated by new climates of thought, bringing different branches of the subject to the fore. Archaeology is no exception to this; an examination of a history of the subject will show that it initially enjoyed close relationships first with geology and evolutionary biology in the late nineteenth century, to be replaced by an emphasis on the study of artefacts (man-made objects) in the early years of this century. This was partly a result of the interest in objects (particularly exotic, valuable objects) stimulated by the great excavations at Ur, Knossos, Troy, Mycenae and the tomb of Tutankhamun, together with a deep-seated fascination with 'old' things and 'ruins' that dates, in England, from the time of the great Tudor and Elizabethan travellers, if not earlier. More recently, in the post-war period, archaeologists have been taking a long, cold look at their subject and trying to find some structure within it.

Archaeology, by its very nature, is an eclectic discipline, meaning that the search for order is made more difficult by the nature of the subject material. The end result has been the enthusiastic, though temporary, adoption of a number of potential methods for finding some order in the chaotic archaeological record, and these academic 'fashions' are neatly represented within the conceptual stratigraphy of the subject. The last, and undoubtedly the most lasting, is called 'environmental archaeology', and is a direct reflection of man's current preoccupation with his modern environment and what is happening to it, together with the rather humbling realisation that man is not, after all, an omnipotent lord of creation but merely one component of his local fauna, with, in many cases, a destructive rather than constructive rôle. The idea of man, and human communities which are, after all, merely collections of men, functioning as part of a total environment has helped archaeologists to interpret their own records, but has necessitated the development of a new series of techniques to recover the buried fragments of ancient human environments. This new 'fashion', requiring, as it does, the assistance of specialists in other scientific disciplines, seems likely to have a great influence on the development of the subject, as it enables archaeologists to move away from examining the sterile remnants of ancient lives and envisage the communities as they actually lived.

Environmental archaeology is concerned both with the reconstruction of these past environments, and with elucidating the rôle and significance of human communities within them. We need to understand the nature of the relationship between man and the land in the past, together with the intrinsic bias imparted by the fragmentary nature of the archaeological record and the processes of change, both natural and human in origin, which the record may reflect. The archaeologist needs to understand how the earth's surface processes function – a vast problem which encompasses all the processes at work during the formation of an archaeological site, including the build-up of sediments (deposition), their removal (erosion) or change (weathering). These processes are shown diagrammatically in fig. 1. The site in question (let us imagine it as a small settlement) accumulates sediments from natural breakdown of local sediments and rocks, as windblown dust or pollen which is carried in the air, and from a wide spectrum of human activities from the domestic to the industrial, and including the construction of houses and all associated buildings. As the sediments accumulate they are constantly mixed by natural agencies varying from earthworms to churning-up by men and animals. Some may be removed, either by natural processes such as flooding and gravity, or by human activities such as the clearing of a new area for building. Even after a site is abandoned (if it ever is) many of these processes can continue. The archaeological deposits which we see today are the result of the interaction of all these complex factors and in order to understand what has happened on the site we need to understand the network of relationships between man, plant, animal and the land itself which is reflected there, enabling us to obtain at least a partial glimpse of early human activities.

The reason for posing such questions on so large a scale must be obvious – that we consider man, or a human community, not in isolation but as a part (and not always a very important part) of a whole ecosystem. Thus, to study the remains of man's past in the 'traditional' way, by looking at the things he has made and fragments of his buildings, is no longer sufficient. These things only represent one aspect of human cultural development. However, with each passing year and with consequent improvements in methodology made by archaeological scientists, the questions which we can ask of the archaeological record become more and more complicated but result in a clearer picture of changing human society. Yet this is not enough; man and his culture need to be set in their constantly changing environmental framework within general parameters of time and space; a framework filled by networks and links which geographers and archaeologists often refer to as 'man-land relationships'. It is necessary for the archaeologist to develop and test theoretical models of such relationships and to understand that each archaeological site or individual fragment of past human activity must be interpreted in its environmental context. Even then, supposing that we are able, assisted by good preservation of plant and animal material (ecofacts), to identify and reconstruct the components of an early environment at a specific date, this is likely to be only possible on a microscopic scale. We might see what the conditions were like in one house, for example, rather than getting

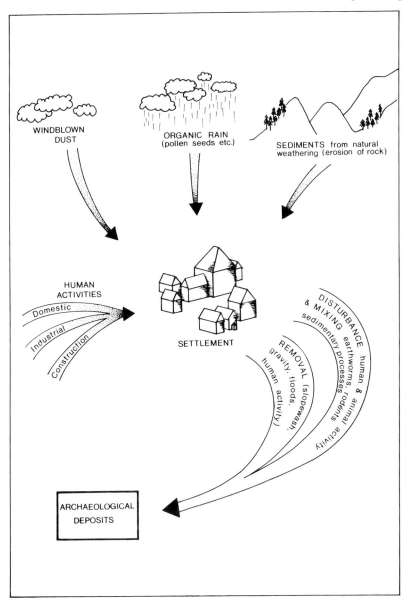

1 Sediments accumulate on a site from different sources, and are then disturbed by various activities. The result, after removal and mixing, is the deposits that we excavate

an overview of life in the whole town. This problem of scale is very difficult to overcome as, inevitably, the excavation coverage of different sites and features is uneven. We know a lot about certain periods and certain sites but virtually nothing about others. This is sometimes the result of differential preservation of information in the archaeological record but may also reflect simpler factors, such as where archaeologists have happened to work or what types of sites are the most obvious. We are therefore a long way from making a large-scale attempt at global environmental archaeology, but must still confine ourselves to reconstructing activities and lifestyles on a very much smaller scale.

Forward-looking archaeologists are trying to solve the problem of scale by studying the archaeology of entire areas and regions rather than individual sites, and from such macroscopic surveys new information is coming about the nature, distribution and character of early life. The hypothetical urban site, referred to above, makes a useful example of this problem of scale. Studying one feature (the remains of a house floor, a storage pit, or a well) at a micro scale will yield interesting information, but only about a comparatively small range of human activities within quite a limited time scale. Large-scale urban excavations at a meso scale will give us comparative data and help us to understand how the town has evolved and what it was like to live there, but a general consideration of the town in its geographical region (the macro scale) will answer much larger-scale questions, such as the type of interaction that took place between the town and its hinterland, what kind of function the town performed at different periods, and how it was linked to other centres by trade and communications networks. It is unfortunately true that the smaller the scale of the question the more information is likely to be available, and to a certain extent this has resulted in a loss of perspective in recent years with archaeologists continually developing better and better techniques to answer smaller and smaller questions, while losing site of the larger frames of reference within which they are working. Synthesis is often frowned upon as being premature, and the postulation of macroscopic questions is discouraged because of the logistical difficulties inherent in working on such a large scale.

There are two ways to approach problems in environmental archaeology, at any scale. The traditional way starts from the individual environmental building-blocks (ecofacts) and considers the methods used for their identification and reconstruction into a fragment of an environment, rather like a jigsaw. This approach is largely the result of the way in which archaeological science has itself developed; the rather piecemeal adoption of new techniques, and their adaptation to archaeological problems, with the result that the methodology has outrun the synthesis and we are left with a lot of data in search of a framework. The new way, pioneered by the American scientist Karl Butzer, is often called the 'systems' approach, and starts by asking questions about human behaviour, trying to construct flow lines for complex situations and explain man-land relationships at the different scales in this way. The central concept, mentioned above, is that of an ecosystem, which makes a framework for studying the different scientific approaches to obtaining information about ecofacts and their interaction. Much of the work is concerned with the development of conceptual models at a very advanced theoretical level which is out of place here, although this book is trying to use a similar approach by presenting the results of environmental analyses as a series of scaled overviews, rather than discussing the methods used to obtain each individual piece of data, and their comparative merits. This avoids the traditional division of environmental archaeology into study areas such as geoarchaeology (sediments, soils, landscapes and surface processes) and bioarchaeology (plant and animal remains), which reflect the training of individual researchers rather than a legitimate division of the subject. Although an archaeologist may have received some training in botany and thus be able to sample and interpret buried plant remains, his view will be limited unless the context of the remains and the scope of their study, together with the scale of the problem, is fully understood. It makes better sense to consider human ecosystems as the basic unit, rather than different categories of ecofact, which will result in a general improvement of perspective and avoid being blinded by technical detail.

One healthy tendency in recent years has been the development of archaeological science as a discipline in its own right, combining the rôles of archaeologist and scientist in one person rather than creating a dichotomy between the people excavating the sites and obtaining the data on the one hand, and the laboratory-based boffins analysing this information (divorced from the site) on the other. However, this is far from being universal. The slowness of environmental archaeology to find a conceptual framework for its data and struggle out from under a mass of individual pieces of information must be seen as the result of lack of contact between site and laboratory workers, partly for logistical reasons and partly as a result of training and experience. Sometimes this has had ludicrous results – the taking of vast amounts of samples from sites with no proper notion of the reason behind such sampling, nor of the questions which might be asked and answered. Sometimes the entomologist or the botanist peering down his microscope will have had little idea of what his information represents in terms of basic elements of a human environment, nor of fundamental questions such as that of scale. One good thing that has come out of this is the publication of extensive series of reports, monographs and books dealing with techniques and methodologies. What we need now is an overview of some of the results and an idea of where we are going in the future.

During the 1970s two important revolutions took place in archaeology; the first connected with the acquisition of data and the second with the way in which the archaeologist made use of it. Inner city redevelopment, motorway construction, deep ploughing, and extensive quarrying operations produced a crisis in British archaeology – the apparent need to 'rescue' large numbers of threatened sites in a fairly uncritical way, often justifying the operations by the argument that it is better to record a little about a lot than the other way round. Funding for research archaeology, and problem-solving site and fieldwork projects, was drastically reduced with the result that much essential perspective was lost and it became increasingly difficult to organise ideas about how all this mass of information could be fitted together. One way of solving the problem was the development of the systematic approach, described above, which endeavoured, through the use of theoretical models, to find a conceptual framework for archaeological research on which to hang all the new data. The idea was intrinsically connected with the development of low-cost computing techniques, initially at university or museum level but now, with the advent of the 'domestic' microcomputer, at the level of individual workers. Another trend was the revival of interest in experimental archaeology – the twentieth-century replication of ancient processes which has proved of vital importance in the study of such matters as site formation processes, animal and plant domestication and early constructional activities.

The need to find methods to deal with the mass of information being produced by the 'rescue' boom also stimulated new advances in dating and analysis techniques for artefacts which, when combined with the idea of considering human communities as components of ecosystems, laid the foundation for the study of socio-economic systems – the remains of cultural activities within their environmental setting. It was realised, very early on, that the nature of the site and the analysis of its data were only part of the problem; archaeologists also needed to concern themselves with the distribution of the archaeological remains in space and time. The location of sites is not random, but occurs as a result of many decision-making factors, perhaps including site function, local topography, availability of resources and microenvironments at the time of habitation. The archaeological record is, unfortunately, always incomplete so that we only have a window on this decision-making process and have to generate hypotheses on less than complete data sets. Not all sites will be equally well preserved, nor will they stand an equal chance of being recovered. This is referred to as 'variations in archaeological visibility' and can be illustrated by an example. Fig. 2a shows a distribution map of Romano-British sites in Northamptonshire, England, recovered as part of a reconnaissance project. The dots on the map mark the location of sites and we are forced to make the *a priori* assumption that the blanks on the map, where there are no dots, must mark places where there are no sites. However, inspection of the second map (fig. 2b) shows that not all areas have been searched for sites, so that the distribution which we see is not 'real' but merely a reflection of archaeological visibility, which in this case is governed by the reconnaissance methods used and the nature of the ground surface. It is clearly impossible to carry out field-walking programmes in heavily built-up or thickly-vegetated areas, which accounts for the lack of dots there. Walking over cultivated fields is much more likely to reveal sites, hence the dots, although if the landscape is developed in clay soils, rather than on limestone

2a

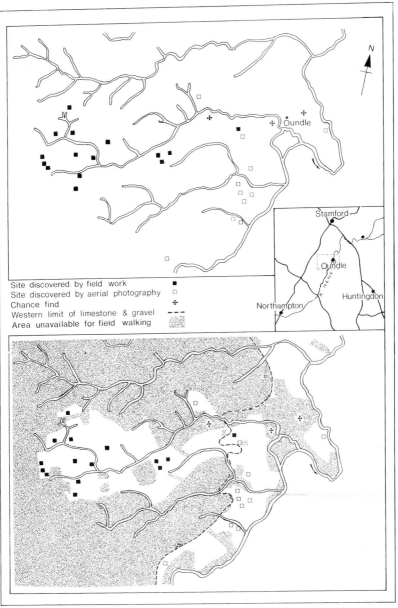

Site discovered by field work   ■
Site discovered by aerial photography   □
Chance find   ✚
Western limit of limestone & gravel   – – –
Area unavailable for field walking

2b

2 The top map shows the distribution of Romano-British sites in part of Northamptonshire, found by different reconnaissance methods. At the bottom we see that the distribution is false; closely related to the type of land surface and its suitability for field survey. After Taylor in Wilson (1975)

or gravels, the sites will not show up from the air. The converse is also true; aerial reconnaissance will show up archaeological sites on lighter soils as soilmarks or cropmarks but is of limited use on heavy clay or thick vegetation. The final site distribution plotted on the map quite possibly bears no resemblance at all to the original distribution of sites in the area but is related to the modern landscape and the reconnaissance techniques used, i.e. to general archaeological visibility. Great caution must therefore be used in the interpretation of distribution maps, which, it has been said (with some truth), may often reflect the distribution of archaeologists rather than sites, perhaps the catchment area of some university or museum field unit.

Students of spatial archaeology have developed models and means of overcoming these problems by statistical techniques but this depends on data availability. For example, it is relatively easy to establish the absolute frequencies of archaeological sites in a semi-desert area which has been well surveyed, where the archaeological visibility is good and where a proper random sampling plan can be worked out. This is not so for an urban redevelopment where the sites will be deep, complex, interrelated and probably never revealed in their entirety or at any one time. In some cases solving problems connected with archaeological visibility can provide a whole new perspective on a culture or a region, as was the case with the distribution of sites associated with the Classic Maya people who flourished in Central America between the period 500–900 AD. In the area of Tikal, Guatamala, American archaeologists used radar imagery and infra-red photography from aircraft to investigate the land use of the Classic Maya. The results showed that the thick jungle cover of the area concealed a series of vast canal networks, some large and widely-spaced and some apparently forming the boundaries for ancient fields. This discovery is of great importance, since beforehand archaeologists, with an absence of evidence to the contrary, had been obliged to speculate that the complex civilization of the Maya, with its huge ceremonial centres (such as Tikal itself) had been based on shifting agriculture rather than settled farming. This seemed very unlikely, and with the discovery of the extensive canal networks the whole picture changed, and it appeared that the Maya were, in fact, the largest-scale users of intensive agriculture in Central America. The swamps, which had formerly appeared to the archaeologists as wasteland, were now realised to be assets, and experiments were carried out to show just how productive cultivation using such a system would have been. In fact, it seems that all the Maya ceremonial centres are located near the edge of swamps, with the canals functioning as highways to transport commodities and building materials. At the height of its power Tikal had an estimated population of more than 50,000 people, but in the absence of good ground reconnaissance, archaeologists had been completely unable to explain how they fed themselves or how their great centres were linked together, until the canal system was revealed from the air.

On a micro scale excavation techniques also govern archaeological

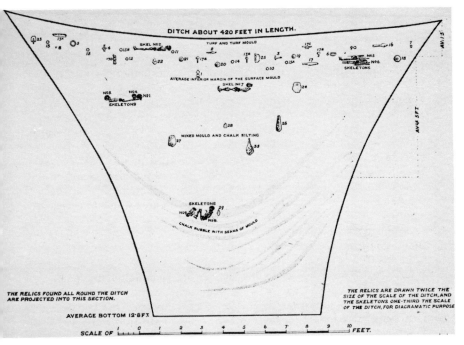

3 Section through the ditch at Wor Barrow, taken from General Pitt-Rivers' *Excavations at Cranborne Chase*.

Note the precise way in which he has located the finds, and given some idea what the ditch silts looked like

visibility, for artefacts, ecofacts and structures. This was realised 100 years ago by General Pitt-Rivers, in his programme of excavations on his extensive (30,000 acres) home estate of Cranborne Chase, Dorset, England, where he developed a systematic method of excavation involving the precise location of all finds and the accurate surveying and drawing of sections, which was way ahead of his time. He may even be credited with some of the first developments in environmental archaeology, notably the keeping of animal bones found during the course of his work, and the initiation of experimental archaeology by killing cattle and comparing their bones with the excavated examples to obtain information about available meat weight. Fig. 3 shows a section through the ditch of Wor Barrow which he excavated in 1893–4. It is remarkable not only for the precisely noted position of all the finds, but also for the unusual attention paid to depicting the sedimentary sequence of the great ditch. His accurate plans and sections were all in advance of their time and in many ways his was the formative influence in changing excavation from a gentlemanly hobby to a scientific exercise. His major work, *Excavations at Cranborne Chase*, was privately published in four huge volumes between 1887 and 1898 and merits close inspection, if for no better reason than that the work certainly qualifies as the first coffee-table book, the huge volumes being admirably suited to this purpose if adapted by the simple addition of legs.

Of course excavation techniques have progressed considerably since his day, through the efforts of innovators such as Sir Mortimer Wheeler (1890–1976) who invented the grid system for sitework and stressed the importance of stratigraphic interpretation and the three-dimensional location of finds, and later techniques of large-scale area excavation relying on a combination of precise planning combined with strategic sections, developed in response to large, complex sites often constituting a 'rescue' problem. It was soon realised that the techniques for the extraction of artefacts and ecofacts from their sedimentary matrices must also be improved, and this led to the development of large-scale 'dirt-processing' methods from the 1970s onwards. Pioneering studies done in the 1970s showed that, even under well-controlled excavation conditions, normal recovery of different artefacts was severely biased, and a series of experiments was set up to examine the extent of this bias and see how it could be avoided. Some of these 'dirt-processing' methods are described below (p. 52), as they produce the large numbers of small ecofacts (bones, seeds, shells etc.) which, when added together, form the remains of human diet. Sieving techniques like that shown in fig. 4, a simple frame sieve with the residues being sorted, have to be adapted to suit different site conditions. Loose, sandy sediments such as those found in Africa and Near Eastern sites where 'dirt-processing' was first invented, can be processed by dry-sieving, either using hand-held sieves of different patterns or sieves mounted on a frame. Clay-rich sediments may need to be wet-sieved (p. 53), often using some means of recycling the water, and further work has shown that even the sieve mesh size can be crucial. Although desirable it is generally impossible to sieve all the residues from an excavation, which necessitates the use of some kind of sampling strategy on the part of the excavator, who must decide what fraction of the matrix can be processed according to the availability of equipment, cash and manpower, and to variations in number and type of context observed. Allowances must be made for different activity areas or occupations, as it will be possible to get answers at different scales and in different degrees of detail from, for example, storage pits or the debris of some industrial activity.

Dirt-processing is vital if adequate samples of ecofacts are going to be obtained. Pitt-Rivers, in his early work, found quantities of bone belonging to the large mammals but no remains of small mammals, birds, fish or microfauna. This is simply a result of the difference in bone size – the smaller the bone, the more difficult it is to see. Without sieving, sometimes needing a very fine mesh (c. 1mm), small bones will not be recovered and it will prove impossible to obtain an unbiased picture of the total range of variations of species utilised by man, perhaps as food sources, or simply as recovery of all the individual building-blocks of this ecosystem. We can thus study site contexts, at different levels of scale, but also need to understand how these

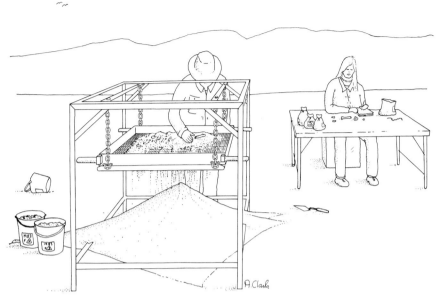

4 Dry-sieving is suitable for loose, sandy deposits. After the sieve has been sorted each find must be marked and recorded

contexts may have been modified by natural or human agency. Comparatively little work has been done on how archaeological sites actually form; this is surprising since the site is composed of 99 per cent sediment which contains the 1 per cent of artefacts, ecofacts and structures used for the reconstruction of culture. People themselves, and the result of their activities, are one of the major agencies in site formation, bringing material to the site, making artefacts or structures there, processing and consuming organic raw materials for food, fuel, clothing and other purposes. The residue of these activities may be enormous if it is left intact, which is why *in situ* deposits, such as those of medieval York (p. 106), may reach great depths and present great problems of interpretation. However, few contexts have remained unchanged since their deposition unless, by some lucky chance analogous to the processes of fossilisation, they were rapidly sealed soon after formation. Examples of such phenomena are buried soils: complete fragments of an early landscape sometimes found sealed under earthworks, such as linear banks or burial structures.

But this type of undisturbed surface is rare, and survives only because it is quickly sealed by the construction of the burial monument. On an occupation site the land surface would rapidly become churned up and disturbed by human and animal activity, with people constantly adding and subtracting sediments and structures in accordance with changing needs and fashions. This debris combines with natural agencies of deposition. The so-called *tell* sites found in the Near and Middle East are monuments to these complex processes, being themselves the result of thousands of years of building on the same site using mudbrick as a major raw material. Mudbrick houses, with a limited lifespan (even when the walls are plastered) collapse with regrettable frequency and it is often far simpler merely to tidy up the debris of one's house and build again on the same site, rather than move completely. Over the centuries a sizeable mound will result, looking like a natural hill, and containing not only thousands of house remains but all the other complex organic and inorganic by-products of human activity together with additions of natural sediment. Çatal Hüyük in Anatolia, described on p. 94, is an example of such a *tell*.

Opportunities to investigate whole sites, or even fractions of a site which are representative of its area and chronological range are, unfortunately, very rare. Archaeologists have to rely on the 'windows' on early occupation which may be produced from only a small excavation, although all are now agreed on the necessity for careful planning, the excavation of representative samples of sites, and the systematic combination of the evidence which they produce, if any really reliable data is to be obtained at a micro scale. However, in many cases interesting information about one aspect of early life may be found from looking at individual houses, or even from the remains of structures (perhaps a well, or cesspit) within them. This will not give us a clear idea of what life was like for the whole community, but will illuminate some small fraction of it, at one moment in time. If we are lucky we may be able to combine the evidence from several sites to increase our range and scope. A survey of the type of picture we could get from such investigations could be carried out in one of several ways; we could look, for example, at the different types of context, or at different types of evidence, different countries or different periods. The approach chosen in this book has been to select a series of topics about which a great deal of evidence has been preserved, which thus illuminate varied facets of early life. This encompasses sites from many different periods and from widely spaced geographical localities and thus enables us to gain at least some idea of the total range of the evidence. We are, I suppose, looking through some bioarchaeological 'windows' onto the ancient world; the frames may be of different sizes but this just helps us to gain some idea of the diversity of the evidence provided by each view.

2
Hunting

We know quite a lot about the diet of modern hunter-gatherer communities from ethnographic observations but of course the archaeological record is heavily biased, because of preservation difficulties, in favour of animal foods. Thus it used to be thought that ancient hunter-gatherers lived almost exclusively on meat. Such an assumption has now been shown quite clearly to be wrong, but it formed the basis for the picture of aggressive meat-hungry cavemen which remained a common impression of what early society was like for some time. In 1957 the venerable palaeontologist Raymond Dart published a paper in which he claimed, after an analysis of over 7,000 bones from the assemblage at Makapansgat Cave in the Northern Transvaal (fig. 5), South Africa, that one of the earliest hominids, *Australopithecus africanus*, was responsible for the vast accumulation of bones at the site some three million years ago, and that the bones represented his food refuse. Thirty years later such an assumption seems rather surprising since we know that australopithecines were small, inoffensive ape-like creatures who might well have had considerable difficulty in killing the large and dangerous animals such as leopard whose bones were incorporated into the Makapan deposits. Dart also noticed that the bones included a large number of skull fragments and interpreted this as the remains of head hunting. His paper, in which he proposed exotic uses for the bone remains which were apparently missing from the deposits (missing tail vertebrae interpreted as animal tails being used for signal flags or whips, and antelope humeri as bludgeons), provoked much thought among anthropologists which progressed along two main lines. Firstly, it stimulated the development of the science of taphonomy to discover exactly how bones did get into archaeological layers, and secondly it made anthropologists think carefully about the diet of early man. Were these first hominids really big-game hunters? It seemed unlikely, yet some people thought that meat-eating was one of the main traits which distinguished man from the apes, and that hunting (with all that it implies in the way of social co-operation, tool-using and food-sharing) was the crucial factor in the separation of the ape and human lines.

Many of these suggestions have now been disproved by later work; chimpanzees, for example, are known (as the result of the work of Jane Goodall) not only to eat meat but occasionally to kill small birds and animals. We also know that hominids apparently became upright-walking perhaps a

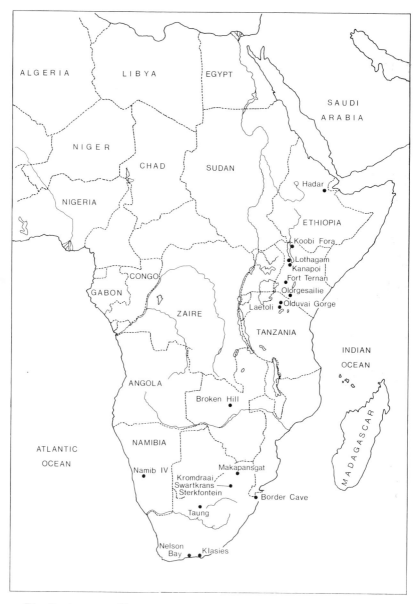

5 Distribution map of hunter-
gatherer sites mentioned in the text

million years before the first tools were made, so that the connection was not causal. But much remains to be learnt about early hominid diet and the only sources of information are to be found in Africa, either in the extensive 'open-air' sites of East Africa, where the remains of hominid meals more than a million years old have survived, or from South Africa, where the fossil remains of early hominids are found, along with the bones of many other animals, in the cave breccias of sites such as Makapansgat (above), Sterkfontein, Swartkrans and Kromdraai near Johannesburg (fig. 5). Dart's ideas have recently been thoroughly tested by Bob Brain, Director of the Transvaal Museum, who has completed ten years' work on these cave sites and concluded not only that many different agencies were responsible for the accumulation of the bones, but also that, far from being the remains of mighty hunters, some of the hominid bones actually constituted the remains of something else's meals.

Brain concluded that the australopithecine bones in the three Sterkfontein Valley caves were the result of carnivore activity – that they represented discarded food remains in much the same way that the bones of baboons (very common in these deposits) did. The australopithecines were quite common at these sites, 140 individuals having been found, of which more than half were sub-adult. Brain considers that they were either the prey of the large cats, especially the leopard, or else of hyaenas. The 'leopard hunting' hypothesis was first generated more than ten years ago when Brain speculated that during the accumulation of the first fossil-bearing deposit at Swartkrans, trees would be able to survive in the shelter of the cave entrances (in contrast to the bleak surrounding savannah) and provide convenient 'larders' for generations of leopards, who tend to hang their prey over the branches of trees to protect them from hyaenas. So, the remains of that prey, be it baboon or australopithecine, gradually become incorporated into the cave sediments. One australopithecine child (specimen SK54 from Swartkrans) had, indeed, apparently got the marks of carnivore incisor teeth in his forehead. However, since his original study, Brain has developed some reservations about the idea. He believes that the bones in the caves (which include those of some bovids far too large to have been eaten by leopards) were probably the result of accumulation by several different carnivores, and that the little australopithecines could have fallen prey to any of them. His second reservation stems from the extraordinarily high proportion of primates in the deposits – more than 50 per cent of the large animals represented in the first layer, Swartkrans Member 1, were either baboons or australopithecines. In normal circumstances primates are not an especially important part of leopard diet unless they are caught while sleeping, so maybe the shallow recesses of the cave were used as sleeping hollows (behaviour common in the Transvaal baboon populations today) which were hunted by carnivores living in the interior of the cave. Either way, at Swartkrans the hominids seem to have been the losers, although the situation gradually changed.

At the nearby cave of Sterkfontein two layers, Members 4 and 5, are especially important for the study of human evolution. During the accumulation of Member 4 the situation in the cave seems to have been rather similar to that of Swartkrans, with cats and hyaenas in control, but by the succeeding Member 5 much more evolved hominids, equipped with fire and tools, had become the hunters. The zoologist Elizabeth Vrba suggests that they were not especially competent, arguing that the nature of the antelope bone remains implies that the first men were scavenging the kills of the large carnivores before they took up hunting for themselves. The Member 5 material is directly associated with stone tools and some of the bones show cut marks. Indeed, the remarkably dense artefact concentrations suggest that the cave was possibly intensively occupied during this phase and that much of the associated bone represents hominid food debris. As well as some small antelopes they include the monitor lizard, and tortoise remains which, as we will see later (p. 45), are common menu items in the later Stone Age and with modern day Bushman communities. The gradual development of prowess in hunting, linked to social and physical evolution, is certainly a manifestation of human success. The little australopithecines never learnt to make tools, nor did they hunt. One variety (*Australopithecus robustus*), so common at Swartkrans, was almost certainly exclusively vegetarian although its lightweight cousin (*Australopithecus gracilis*, or *Australopithecus africanus* as it is often known) found at Sterkfontein, seems to have eaten anything that came his way. We know that both varieties survived alongside the early representatives of *Homo* for perhaps millions of years, occupying different ecological niches, but their ultimate lack of success (signified by their extinction) must be partly attributed to the fact that, unlike *Homo*, they never learned to take the initiative.

Modern taphonomic work at Makapan suggests that the exotic osteodontokeratic proposals for australopithecines made by Dart must be replaced by a scenario involving the selective accumulation of bones by hyaenas and, most importantly, by porcupines, who, although vegetarians themselves, need hard objects to chew in order to wear down the edges of their front teeth. Bones fulfil this function splendidly and also contribute phosphorus and calcium to the porcupine's diet (fig. 6). Other agents which add bones to caves are, in later periods, man (as food remains) and owls, from their regurgitated pellets which are readily recognisable since they are rich in microfauna such as moles, voles and insects.

Many of the 'open-air' (as opposed to cave) sites where there are also preserved remnants of hominid activity differ very greatly from most people's idea of a conventional archaeological site. The so-called 'living floors' at African sites such as Olorgesailie, Olduvai and Kalambo Falls (fig. 5) may be mere collections of stone artefacts (sometimes accompanied by bone) which represents the debris of very short-term occupation, or indeed not of occupation at all, in the strict sense of the word, but rather of some specific function such as the killing or butchery of an animal. Such localities present

6 Bones accumulate in caves through various agencies, both animal and human. Owls will contribute regurgitated pellets and hyaenas parts of their scavenged prey. People, like porcupines, bring in a lot of non-food debris and modify the cave environment considerably

many problems in interpretation, and recent work has upset our ideas about the activities of early man, and his relationship with other animal components of his environment. There are numerous 'hunting' sites where archaeologists have examined the bone remains from kill sites to evaluate not only the amount of animals killed and the resulting meat weight, but its nutritive value. In order to do this it is necessary to understand the complex relationship between the numbers of animals originally killed (the so-called 'death assemblage') and the small fraction of this which is preserved in the archaeological record, after all the processes of selective decay and the biases introduced by human selection of certain parts of animals have been introduced. The study of this series of processes is called taphonomy and, together with experimental replication of archaeological processes (p. 152), is one of the most important fields in contemporary archaeological science. It is, however, quite a new one, pioneered by scientists like Kay Behrensmayer who were faced with extracting some meaning from all the bone assemblages associated with the remains of early forms of men in East African sites like Koobi Fora or Olorgesailie (fig. 5). Observation has had to be combined with experiment. Fig. 7a shows a goat skeleton which was the subject of an early experiment carried out by Bob Brain to examine this question of survival. He observed the way in which Hottentots living near the River Kuiseb in

7a

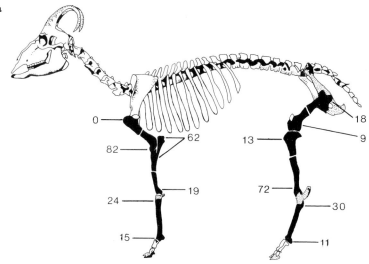

7b

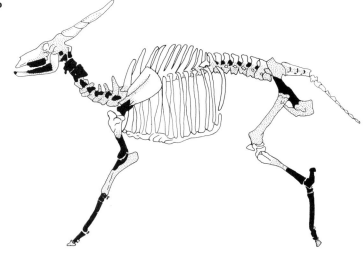

Namibia butchered a goat and also collected goat bones from the area, looking at the survival of different parts of the body. The diagram shows the ways in which the different ends of the long bones survived; this varied with the durability of the different parts, and whether or not they were chewed by people or dogs. Taking the humerus, for example, 82 distal ends were found from a sample of 2,373 goat pieces representing a minimum of 190 animals, but not a single proximal end. In fig. 7b we see the result of Bob Brain's later work, an antelope skeleton where the various parts of the body have been allocated 'potential survival ratings'. The parts shown in black, including parts of the jaw, pelvis, vertebrae and lower limbs, have the highest potential for survival, stippled elements (horn cores, other vertebrae) have intermediate ratings, and the unshaded bones (ribs etc.) are most unlikely to survive at all.

This type of work is leading to a number of different (and inevitably conflicting) interpretations of early hominids' food remains, and of the activities which they represent. Some archaeologists, such as Glyn Isaac, suggest that the early hominids threw away both bone and stone at their home bases, and shared food. Several different types of sites are recognised, notably the classification of Olduvai Gorge sites, excavated by Mary Leakey, into living floors (with shallow occupational debris), butchery/kill sites (where stone tools are associated with animal bones), and different types of sites where the material may be associated but has been extensively disturbed. A great deal of speculation has been carried out about how hominids organised themselves, often involving the back-projection from ethnographic observations of modern hunter-gatherers as well as analogies made with other primates. Nobody really knows. Lewis Binford looked at the material from Olduvai Gorge and came to a different conclusion saying that several different agencies were responsible for the accumulations, rather than different activities. Some bone assemblages closely paralleled the structures of wolf kill assemblages in their patterns of the destruction and survival of bone. Others indicated that animal gnawing had been more important than men breaking down the bones for marrow. Few, he concluded, were the results of hominid kills of large animals and he suggested that these large sites, although crucial in that they provide actual hominid fossils to enable us to reconstruct some of the earliest stages of our evolution, actually tell us very little about how our ancestors behaved. The bones suggest that the large bovids, say, were killed by carnivores, and the carcass then rapidly became disarticulated and scattered by other predators. In fact, the most common bones in the assemblages are not those which would have had high food

7 Different parts of the body do not have equal 'archaeological visibility'. Bob Brain, working on Hottentot goat bones (a) noted that some parts survived well while others were totally absent, and that some bones (e.g. bits of jaw and pelvis) were likely to survive better than others (ribs). The antelope skeleton (b) shows the bits that vanish

utility but they would have yielded marrow, which was probably being scavenged from the carcasses by the hominid tool makers, although they themselves had not done the killing. The stone tool assemblages, dominated by bashing and breaking tools, support this and suggest that the hominids were not hunters but opportunistic scavengers exploiting the kills of more successful carnivores. The bones also suggest that not much meat was removed, eradicating the picture of hunters bringing home meat supply to their families at some home base far away from the kill. This makes a much less attractive picture but is probably closer to the truth.

Animal bones will not survive everywhere. Very quick burial under sediments which remain moist (excluding the bacteria which cause decay) or rapid drying out of the bone are the best conditions for preservation. On open-air sites bone residues are likely to be affected by all sorts of natural processes of disturbance including wind, water and animal activity before they become incorporated into archaeological deposits. This means that the relationship between the preserved bones and the stone tools with which they are frequently associated may not be as simple as it appears. Bones preserved in caves or rock shelters have a much higher survival rate, but are again subject to different sorts of bias. There is a clear relationship between the nature of the burial environment and the structure of the bone assemblage that survives. Thus, because bones are plentiful on one site and absent on another this does not mean that no hunting took place on the former, but it might reflect the disturbance of the site or unfavourable preservation conditions. Similarly, as we shall see, because the bones of one species seem to predominate on a particular site this does not necessarily mean that that species was the most commonly hunted. All sorts of other factors could be responsible, and to sort them out is the task of the taphonomist.

When the first palaeolithic sites were found, with a combination of stone tools and animal bone, it was natural for the archaeologist to assume that the animal bones represented the remains of hunting activities, but this need not necessarily be the case. A famous example of this can be seen at the sites of Torralba and Ambrona in southern Spain, where, around 350,000 years ago, a group of one of the hominid ancestors of modern man known as *Homo erectus* had apparently taken advantage of an area of boggy ground at the edge of a lake, driven elephants down from the foothills, perhaps using fire, waited until they were trapped and then killed, butchered and eaten them. The remains of this activity, elephant bones associated with stone tools, could be clearly seen and the site was considered especially important since it appeared to prove co-operation between hominid groups at rather an early date, as well as some means of communication and the ability to plan and execute game drives. Unfortunately, this attractive hypothesis has recently been reassessed. Only 611 tools were found at Torralba, within a deposit which might have taken thousands of years to form. A radical reappraisal of the evidence from the site suggests that despite its reputation as a large-scale hunting site only 115 animals were, in fact, killed of which 31 per cent were elephants. If the deposits took 10,000 years to form, this gives the death rate of 1 animal per 87 years and makes the 'game drive' idea seem unlikely. It is indisputable that many of the skeletal parts of elephants are missing and that the skeletal remains are frequently associated with butchery tools. But can we assume from this evidence that the hominids were actually responsible for the death of these animals, much less driving them? It is an attractive idea, made especially agreeable by the general absence of evidence for the social organisation of early hunting communities, and the picture of co-operative big game hunting is appealing. But is it true? Surely a far more likely explanation is that the animals died there naturally and were scavenged. We cannot make the assumption that every bone associated with tools is the remains of a hunter's kill. The archaeological facts at Torralba are the stone tools; we need to consider other elements before we interpret what activities they represent.

One can illustrate this point by an archaeological site which is arguably the earliest and most exciting ever found, that of the trail of footprints made by a pair of hominids walking across hard volcanic ash at Laetoli in East Africa some three and a half million years ago. The footprint trail (which clearly showed that the hominids were upright-walking) was found by Mary Leakey, together with the tracks of many other animals and birds ranging from elephants to ostriches, which had also been sauntering across the ash deposits. Yet we do not automatically assume that all these animals were being hunted by the owners of these first human footprints, merely that they happened to be living in the same area. Analysis of the tracks shows us that the countryside was rich in big game (giraffe, elephant), but also had smaller animals equally familiar to us today, such as guinea-fowl, ostrich, hares and various insects, some of which might indeed have been eaten by early man and all of which may be used to reconstruct his environment. So how do we actually decide what was eaten and what was not?

Easily the most important research project ever undertaken in order to resolve this and related questions is the work of Lewis Binford (inevitably) among the Nunamiut Eskimo, which involved observations carried out between 1969 and 1972, the analysis of 122,000 bones known to be the result of Nunamiut activities, and the observation of more than 400 episodes of butchery with step-by-step recording of the procedures. This immense archive of information has been applied by Binford to some archaeological bone assemblages already excavated, in order to try and understand what really happened; to see, as it were, the sequence of events which took place between the time in which the animal was killed and the appearance of its bones in the course of an excavation. Only in this way can we understand how hunters really operated or whether, indeed, they were hunters at all, or merely predator-scavengers. Binford's work helps in all sorts of ways – the identification of precise butchery marks, for example, that reflect skinning or dismemberment. He observed the pattern of cut marks made on a skull by the Nunamiut when the carcasses which they were butchering were frozen or very stiff from having been dead for some time. Identical patterns of cut marks were found on antelope skulls which had been butchered by neanderthals at the middle palaeolithic site of La Quina in France. He also noticed that the modern Nunamiut took very great pains when skinning out the feet of animals, leaving a distinct pattern of cut marks, since they were anxious to preserve the skin for the manufacture of mukluks (skin boots) and skin socks. Similar marks were also observed at La Quina (noted in the important study of butchery marks from that site made at the very early date of 1907–1910 by Henri Martin) and it is far from improbable that Neanderthals were equally concerned with their footwear. Stone tools leave a whole variety of marks on bone – evidence of chopping, bone breakage and the selective dismemberment of carcasses for specific purposes or for favoured joints of meat. However, it is impossible to interpret such evidence without the aid of modern experimental replication of ancient techniques, combined with ethnographic observation. Very few hunter-gatherer communities today still use stone tools; Binford's observations of Eskimo showed butchery with metal tools, yet he was able to make some comparison with stone butchery marks. Professor Otto Köhler, who has carried out a 25-year study project on one group of Kalahari Bushmen (still technically a 'Stone Age' people) told me that he had only once seen a stone tool being used; pieces of metal (often acquired from metal fencing) having replaced stone in everything from arrowheads to butchery knives.

In 1964 an expedition to the Baynes Mountains area of northern Namibia photographed and recorded the use of stone tools by hunter-gatherer OvaTjimba tribesmen who still live in the area today. Even here, the OvaTjimba said that they preferred to use iron when they could get it and one member of the group was seen to cut up his meat with the lid of a beer can instead of using a stone tool. The opportunity was taken to record the whole process of stone tool use, from selection of the raw material through preparation of the tool and details of which tools were selected for which jobs. The quartz flakes which were photographed being used by one member of the group, named Kaupatana, to skin a springbok, are in the course of detailed examination at the time of writing. Such studies give us an insight into how early communities actually prepared their kills, and are very valuable in making an interpretation of the archaeological record.

Useful information may often be gained by comparisons made between the bone assemblages from different hunter-gatherer sites, especially if they come from roughly the same period. Bones from the famous mesolithic (Middle Stone Age) site of Star Carr in Yorkshire have been compared with bones from other European mesolithic sites including Kongenmosen, Praestelyngen and Muldbjerg 1 in Denmark. It was found that the bone assemblages were markedly different, notably in the ways that specific bones had been utilised by these early post-glacial hunters for their marrow. The pattern of bone cracking for marrow observed at Praestelyngen and Muldbjerg 1 was very similar to that noted by Binford working with the

Nunamiut at their long-term residential camps, whereas at Star Carr the pattern of breaks was of a type observed when frozen carcasses were being prepared. The very low frequency of femurs (thigh bones) at Star Carr, together with other factors suggested that the site was a kill-butchery location or a field camp, rather than a long-term occupation site; a hypothesis which was supported by other biological evidence.

There is no evidence that the hominids at Olduvai were hunting. The best sites, such as the elephant kill site coded FLK North Level 6, perhaps the large semi-articulated animals at HWK East Level 2, and the hippo location at Koobi Fora are likely natural death locations. The tools at the kill sites at both Olduvai and Olorgesailie are localised largely independently of the bones, but this is not so at Namib IV (p. 37) and other, later, sites belonging to *Homo erectus*. We think that the earliest tools were for cutting and butchering animals, enabling hominids to become more effective at scavenging. Tool-making and hunting do not, it appears, arrive at the same time and man later became more successful at killing on his own account. Some people see this early concentration on obtaining bone marrow as being man using tools to take advantage of an opportunity which no other animal, it seems, was using. Bearing in mind the importance of fat in the human diet this is very possible. Early hominids looking for bone marrow and equipped with crushing tools had the advantage of every other species, except hyaenas, and ecological success is bestowed upon those with advantages.

It may be that we have to dispense with a number of favourite illusions, such as the rise of big game hunting with *Homo erectus*, since it has been claimed that regular successful scavenging would inevitably result in a numerical shift towards larger animals which have more meat remaining, although there is no proof of this. However, all this work on bone assemblages certainly suggests that our idea of man the hunter must be revised, if not abandoned, until some later stage in human prehistory.

Additional and supporting evidence about the way in which bone remains may be used in the interpretation of behaviour comes from many palaeo-indian sites in America which again show that great efforts were made to extract bone marrow. The Garnsey bison kill site, located on the eastern edge of the Pecos River Valley in New Mexico, is a well-documented kill site left by the Great Plains Indians. The bones were examined by John Speth, with the object of reconstructing their nutritional value. He was trying to understand the processes which lead early man to choose, butcher and process only certain animals from a herd, and how these choices can be reconstructed from the archaeological records. Speth's approach was important since he emphasised that not only were the seasonal conditions of animals an important factor in choice (with bison these differences favour the killing of bulls in the spring and cows in the autumn and winter) but that seasonality also affected the use of an animal, how it was butchered and what parts were removed from the kill site. It is quite common now for archaeologists to evaluate the sex structure of animal kills which, when taken together with

8 A North American bison

other items of evidence like tooth wear and eruption, can tell the season when the hunt was made. Sexing of bison (fig. 8) is generally done from skulls, or, if intact examples are not well preserved, from jawbones or footbones. Plains bison-hunters needed animals of both sexes for different purposes. Cow skins were used for robe-making and containers while the thicker tough bull hides made bowstrings, soles for moccasins, shield covers and had many other uses. All parts of the bison were useful not only for food but in ritual and the wide range of material equipment from tents to glue that was required.

The custom of selectively hunting animals of different sexes at different times of the year when they were in their prime was both logical and well established and it would be customary, for example, to hunt bulls in the late spring and early summer when they were in prime condition but avoid them during and after the rutting season when their condition was much poorer. At the Garnsey site not only were the majority of remains from bulls, but the few cows that had been killed were hardly butchered at all, with the result that most of the bones left behind came from cows, not bulls, although far more of the latter had been killed. Speth wondered why. The animals that had been left behind were in very poor condition, often being pregnant cows or animals still feeding young, and there had been selective removal of those bones richest in fat. This indicated that the Indians valued fat highly, as many hunting communities do, abandoning (or avoiding) thin animals. The hunters were highly selective in the animals that they killed and the parts of those animals that they chose to eat. Bison kill sites generally contain mostly females, which archaeologists have taken to suggest that more females than males were killed (assuming that their carcasses received identical butchery treatment and thus had equal chances of being reflected in the archaeological record). Speth's analysis of the Garnsey material showed that this was not true at all; in the initial kill (which was dominated by bulls) certain male elements were preferentially removed into dumps of bones in which the remains of females predominated, which completely changes the picture.

The mound of bison bones at Garnsey had been incorporated into alluvial deposits, but radio-carbon dating of the bones suggested that it represented quite a short time span. Kills spanned less than 200–300 years around 500–450 BP, within the late prehistoric period and before the introduction of horse or gun, and constituted individual 'events' of varied sizes where between 4 and 20 animals were killed at any one time.

After butchery (by various stone flake tools) the carcasses became piles of almost 7,000 totally disarticulated bones. Data from the animals' teeth and jaws gave the Minimum Number of Individuals (MNI) represented (35), the age and sex of this population and the season when they were killed. Some very curious contradictions were observed; based on skulls, males outnumbered females by 60/40, but the same calculation based on below-skull (postcranial) evidence suggests the reverse – that females outnumbered males by 66/34. This disparity could be the result of the removal of female skulls from the kill site for some reason but it seems unlikely since skulls were fairly useless anyway. Speth considered that the skulls represent the sex ratio of the original population, 60/40 in favour of males when all the kill events are combined. It seems that the hunters carefully considered the age and state of each carcass before butchery, and those parts of the female carcasses which were low in fat were abandoned. The bison was simply so abundant that it was possible for fifteenth-century Plains Indians to ignore large proportions of the important marrow bones from pregnant or lactating cows as the same bones on other animals which were killed would provide more fat. This is a far cry from our common picture of hunting communities utilising their kill down to the last hair – apparently, when animals were plentiful, they have no need to do so.

Such observations tell us about aspects of Indian life and hunting practices which could be obtained from no other source except the painstaking analysis of thousands of bones. The element of opportunism, either in scavenging other animals' kills or in lying in wait at suitable kill sites can seldom have been absent in early hunting strategies. Sometimes, indeed, the evidence is merely sitting on the surface of the ground as is the case at the site of Namib IV, located in what is at present one of the most forbidding spots on the globe, the Central Namib desert (fig. 9). In the Namib, as in many deserts, the remains of very early human activity may be found lying around on the surface, and at Namib IV the reason for this is easy to see as the stone tools, dominated by a magnificent series of large heavy-duty kill and butchery tools (fig. 10), were incorporated into surface deposits soon after their abandonment, together with the remains of the animals which had been killed. The

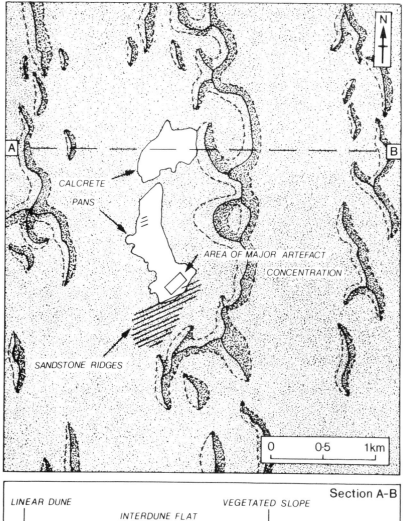

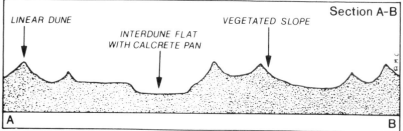

9 The artefacts and bones at Namib IV were scattered over an interdune flat where there had been a waterhole, half a million years ago. The pan lies in the middle of high linear sand dunes in the Central Namib desert

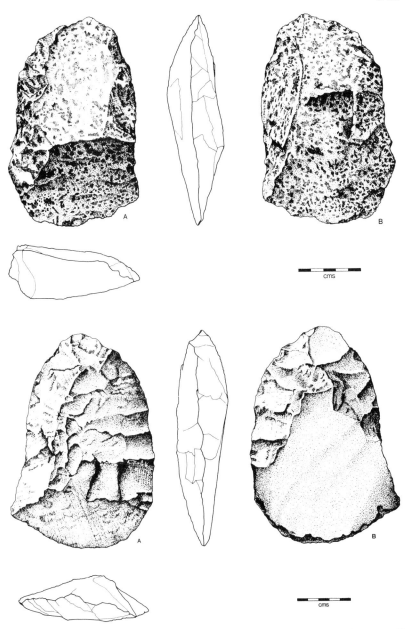

10 Two examples of the heavy-duty cleavers used for butchering elephants at Namib IV. This pair, made of quartzite, both show signs of use (small chips removed from their cutting edges)

11 Elephant tooth fragments from Namib IV. Now completely fossilised, these fragments are being used to date the site, and are more than half a million years old

site appears to have been a water hole at the time of this event, now dated by isotopic decay (Thorium/Argon method) to around half a million years ago, around the same date as Olorgesailie. Namib IV is the first evidence for man in south-west Africa, and it is probable that these early hunters waited for animals to come and drink. The remains of elephant (fig. 11), horse, buffalo and two different bovids were found associated with the tools, completely fossilised but identifiable, although very fragmentary. Only eight animals were represented in the assemblage which seems to be a clear example of a kill site. Several similar localities have now been found in the Namib, all associated with former water-hole localities, where the tools and bone seem likely to have been buried by sand movement soon after their deposition. Fig. 12 shows the minute bone fragments and associated stone tools and charcoal that mark the site where a gemsbok (oryx) was caught and cooked 14,000 years ago. The find of elephant remains from Namib IV in what is now one of the driest areas of the world, thousands of square miles of shifting sand dunes, was very surprising but a similar site is now known from the Kalahari desert. It is possible that the hunters took advantage of game travelling across dry land from one water hole to the other, since in the present day in the northern Namib elephants have been seen to traverse desert areas. Only a relatively small amount of bone and stone was found which could indicate that the site, and ones like it, were only utilised for a short time (which seems probable) and that early man knew of the existence of the water holes and took

12 A mixture of bone splinters, charcoal and stone tools marks where a gemsbok (oryx) was killed 14,000 years ago in the shifting dunes of the Namib

advantage of them. Richard Klein, who has done a great deal of work on the bone assemblages found on African sites noted that elephant bones are almost entirely absent from 'base camps', though butchery sites (such as the famous 'Cutting 10' site at Elandsfontein in the southern Cape) are quite often rich in elephant remains. This would support the idea that Namib IV is a kill/butchery site; indeed, one would hardly envisage early man wishing to spend long in the dunes unless he needed to.

Just up the dune from Namib IV there is another site which tells a rather different hunting story and is, indeed, much later in date. At Rooikamer (fig. 13) a series of 28 hunting blinds, some in the form of circles (fig. 14), were identified alongside game trails leading down from the high dunes of the Namib to cliffs and eventually down to the River Kuiseb which marks the northernmost limit of the Namib sand desert. The circles and stands were very varied in construction but seem to have been located with the object of shooting or spearing game on its way down to drink. Significantly, they were archaeologically sterile and probably used by Late Stone Age hunters to predict the arrival of their meat supply which was then removed to higher ground for butchery. On the higher ground an area of 2,500m² was found covered with ash deposits and stone tool scatters of various periods, suggesting again that the locality had been exploited over some considerable period. The divorce of function between the hunting circles and butchery on higher ground is interesting since carrying a heavy carcass some 100m or so would seem unnecessary; yet the broken ground where the circles were located is full of rock shelters which still harbour a hyaena population,

13 Hunting circles at Rooikamer, both made of fissile schist slabs. The example at the top has been built into the cliff while the bottom one is free standing, near game trails

competition for the kill. Indeed, when working at the site some years ago I was woken on several occasions by the heavy breathing of hyaenas who once took the ultimate liberty of urinating on my tent pole!

Clive Gamble has recently reviewed some of the European cave sites and notes that they are very rich in carnivore remains – up to 45 per cent of the

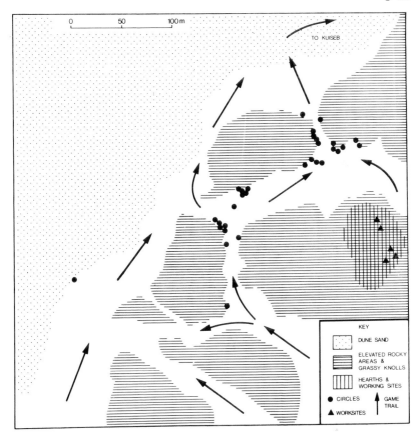

14 Game trails at Rooikamer lead down from dunes to the river. The shelters, archaeologically sterile, were positioned near them but game was carried to the higher ground for butchery

fauna, excluding the very common remains of the cave bear. This is unlikely to be the result of hominids hunting large carnivores and far more likely to represent the animals that naturally lived in small caves and rock shelters. Quite often not many tools are found and long-term occupation is unlikely. This contrasts with open-air sites where the faunas are dominated, not surprisingly, by herbivores. However, the relationship between the large carnivores and man does appear to change towards the end of the palaeolithic with the culture called Magdalenian, after the type-site of La Madelaine in the Dordogne, France. Magdalenian layers in caves have relatively few carnivore remains while earlier layers are quite rich in them. It may be that man, whose population density greatly increased during this time, was able to dominate the large carnivores, not compete with them. It

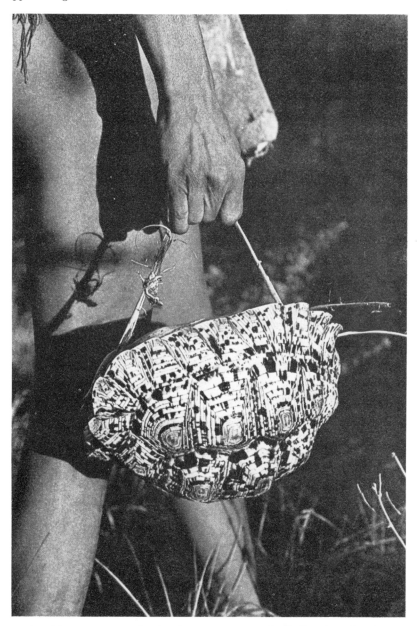

15 Anything, even a tortoise, is grist to a Bushman mill, and after eating its occupant the shell makes a handy container

may, or may not, be significant that carnivores are also relatively uncommon in the cave paintings of that period, which are dominated by representation of the large herd animals (reindeer, mammoth, woolly rhino) which were providing the hunters with their main food source. Most hunting communities get some of their protein food from animals that were gathered, rather than hunted. Tortoise (fig. 15) and shellfish would come into this category, as would the lizards, edible caterpillars, grubs and larvae which make up a substantial part of the diet of many modern hunting communities such as the Bushman. Tortoises, can, perhaps surprisingly, produce interesting archaeological information. At the De Hangen cave in Cape Province the remains of over 300 tortoises were found, which had been used as food by its Late Stone Age inhabitants. Since the tortoises of that area hibernate in the winter, the excavator John Parkington was able to suggest that the cave had been occupied in summer, a contention supported by the fact that the cave deposits also contained plentiful remains of the dassie, or rock hyrax. An age for each specimen was obtained from an examination of its tooth eruption, and, since it is known from modern zoological studies that young dassies are born between September and November, Parkington calculated that all the dassies found could also have been killed during the summer months. A third, clinching piece of evidence was the bedding of the inhabitants, four species of woody plants known to flower between October and December (the South African high summer).

Observations on living hunter-gatherers are of incalculable value. In his study of the !Kung Bushmen of north-west Botswana the anthropologist Richard Lee concluded that only 37 per cent of their diet consisted of meat (fig. 16), the rest being contributed by gathered plants. The stable dietary base of the Bushmen, and other 'hunting' communities is not hunting but gathering; hunting is a subsistence activity which has rather a low return for quite a high risk, whereas gathering relies on food sources which are much more reliable and produce higher returns. Judging from the remains found in African archaeological sites this combination of food obtained by hunting, with food obtained by gathering was also practised in the palaeolithic.

Bushmen use an incredibly wide range of plant foods; one study of the G/wi Bushmen of Central Botswana listed 35 different species of plants utilised for different purposes. Fig. 17 shows a !Nara melon bush in the Namib desert. These !Nara, whose incredibly nutritious seeds are still an important food staple of the local Hottentots today, are found in archaeological sites from the Late Stone Age onwards, and indeed there is a marked correspondence between the location of such sites and the favoured growing localities for !Nara. Such studies on plant foods are valuable because they suggest that it is likely that plants would have been at least as important to early man as they are to Bushmen today – yet they have very low archaeological visibility. The gathering of plant foods is generally the work of the women in a group, simply equipped with a digging stick and some kind of bag for their spoils; neither artefact being likely to survive well. However, with improved techniques for

17 A small protein- and vitamin-rich
!Nara melon growing near the River
Kuiseb, Namibia. These melons have
been used by hunter-gatherers from
the Middle Stone Age to the present
day

the recognition of plant foods we are beginning to gain some idea of what
early man ate. The cave sites of the southern Cape, for example, have
yielded large quantities of plants important to early man. The relatively
dry conditions at Melkhoutboom cave produced well-preserved plant
remains from layers dating as far back as 15500 BP, including roots, corms,
seeds and fruits, many with medicinal as well as seasonal uses and some which
would have been a source of arrow-poisons or mastics for attaching
arrowheads to shafts. The assemblage was dominated by corms of *Watsonia*, a
very widely-available plant food nicknamed 'Hottentots bread', which was
ground and roasted before being eaten. The plant remains were so plentiful
that it was even possible to reconstruct the seasons at which the cave was
occupied, and suggest occupation in the spring and early summer during the
period 7000–3000 BP, when the site seems to have been occupied by people
who were especially reliant on plant foods. The inhabitants of the cave were
probably intimately aware of the potential of all types of plants within their
habitat, and able to predict where certain species would be found, or identify

16 Snakes are another common item
on Bushman menus, and taste rather
like chicken (although they have
rather more attractive skins)

a food plant by a shoot that would be passed over by less acute eyes, in the way observed in modern Bushman communities.

Apart from producing evidence about the diet of the Melkhoutboom cave dwellers we can also get an idea of their environment. The composition of the plant assemblages gradually changes going up the deposits, reflecting a change from forest near the cave to more open habitats near the site towards the end of the occupation when the hunters were collecting plant foods from scrub and savanna areas yet still hunting small browsing antelope in more heavily vegetated environments. Of course, this probably reflects a sexual division of labour as well, which is also supported by recent ethnographic observations. Professor Hilary Deacon, who excavated Melkhoutboom cave, also recorded oral traditions about the movements of the last Bushman band left in the Long Kloof area of the eastern Cape. It consisted of about 16 hunter-gatherers and occupied a series of three caves, one on the coast for about two months in the summer, a second in the hills during the winter and a third in a small tributary river during the rest of the year – making the best of resources which were seasonably available in different environments. South African archaeologists are fortunate in having this type of ethnographic evidence at their disposal – it is a complete contrast to the European situation where, for the first 90 per cent of the Stone Age, undisturbed sites are so rare that it is very difficult to get even the simplest information about the nature and quality of life at the early period. Of course some hunters do survive almost exclusively on meat but this is rare, except in high latitudes where it is common to find diets composed of more than the average 20–45 per cent of hunted food common in such societies.

The Eskimo are a prime example of people who are almost entirely dependent on hunted food. There was a famous experiment carried out by two Arctic explorers in the 1930s, Steffansson and Andersen, who lived for a year on an all-meat diet (under close medical supervision) to test the hypothesis that it was indeed possible for a man to survive without plant foods. Their health remained reasonable as long as they ingested bone marrow (which was their major source of Vitamin C) and balanced out lean and fat meat. The eating of lean meat alone leads to malnutrition and death and the experiment emphasised the importance of fat, confirmed by many ethnographers by observations of Eskimo, Indian and Lapp society. The importance of fat was doubtless well known to early man and may explain, for example, why the hunters at the Garnsey bison-kill site (above, p. 36) simply abandoned lean, fat-depleted animals. Diets high in lean meat are relatively inefficient and may result in hunters having to eat very large quantities of meat or become selective in killing the fattest animals and processing the body parts which are rich in fats. This is important in evaluating the archaeological record, which can no longer simply be done in terms of 'meat weight represented from bones' but must be evaluated from a nutritional point of view. Archaeologically, the discarding of bones which would apparently have been rich in meat may seem wasteful, but such bones may have been capable of contributing relatively little to the diet of the hunters.

Another way for the hunters to get fat is by supplementing their big game hunting at certain times of the year (especially winter and spring) with animals which have high fat contents, like migratory waterfowl such as ducks or geese, beaver, seal, penguin etc., depending on location. Sometimes the hunting of birds was exceptionally successful in the past; in the case of the flightless moa, a large ostrich-like bird living in New Zealand, the Maori hunters caused its extinction, just as the attentions of European hunting societies combined with environmental change had resulted in the extinction of many animal species, including the mammoth. A large research project has recently been mounted by the archaeozoologist Atholl Anderson, to investigate moa hunting in the South Island of New Zealand, since almost nothing is known of its logistics. Moa were extinct before the arrival of the first European settlers and had, some time previously, become so scarce that the moa hunts had almost entirely disappeared from the traditions of the Maori. Careful fieldwork and selective excavation showed that the moa were highland birds living on forest fringes and mixed shrubland, and in that area had provided more than 90 per cent of the meat supply for the Maori hunters during the peak of moa hunting between 850 and 550 BP. Moa hunting was carried out from base camps and a series of shorter term hunting camps, and the moa eggs were gathered from the higher altitude sites in season. The short-term but very intensive hunting of the moa resulted in its disappearance, assisted by human destruction of moa habitats by burning, and the inability of the local vegetations to recover sufficiently quickly. After 400-300 BC bird hunting in the South Island had virtually ceased and was in any case reliant on other, smaller birds.

Societies which destroy their own resource base are rare; as we have seen, most hunters take care to balance supply and demand, developing flexible strategies to adapt their lives to the different resources provided in the course of the seasonal round. The trouble is that archaeologically we may have great difficulty in interpreting these strategies, since the evidence is incomplete. Ethnographic evidence is clearly going to be helpful here, but it may mean losing some precious preconceptions. One can think of many examples of this; the sexual dimorphism in food-gathering exhibited by modern hunter-gatherers, where males tend to range further away from home to hunt but actually contribute less to the general food supply than the females, who have been gathering plant foods nearer home.

Observations made of the Australian aborigines have been especially helpful, since, like the Bushmen, some aboriginal societies still make a living by hunting and foraging in the same areas where a continuity of such occupations carried out by their ancestors is evidenced archaeologically stretching over many thousands of years. A recent case-study illustrates the importance of this approach, and was carried out by the Australian archaeologist Betty Meehan among the Anberra, a 100-strong aboriginal community who live at the mouth of the Blyth river in Arnhem Land, Northern Australia. They are especially interesting since their diet relies heavily on shellfish as a source of protein. As we have already seen, shellfish seldom provide the main protein source for a community but may be a 'supplementary benefit'. It is, however, very difficult to deduce anything about prehistoric shellfish exploitation just from the remains preserved in middens and some very simplistic ideas have been produced. The observations made on the Anberra changed all that. It was found that the Anberra collected shellfish on more than half the days of the year but the numbers of different species collected varied from 1–13 although on most days it was only 1. This matches up quite well with previous observations on middens, which are generally composed mainly of just one species. But is this simply because that mollusc tasted better, or are some other factors at work? The Anberra 'targeted' a species before going out to collect, depending on where they were camped and what time of the year it was. Sometimes enthusiastic 'targeting' resulted in a shellfish bed becoming exhausted, in which case the Anberra changed species until their preferred one had recovered. They carefully planned their foraging and there was no element of random selection, even if the species were apparently of equal edibility.

This apparent preference for one species over another has also been noted before, and put down to dietary preferences. However, if the species to be gathered that day was already decided upon, why did the deposits which contained the remains of the day's activities always include a certain element of 'untargeted' species? An answer to this question might help in interpreting the small percentage of minor species found in archaeological middens. The answer, surprisingly, lay in aspects of the behaviour of the community. Children would collect several species rather than the chosen one, or forage in the intertidal zone where shells were thin on the ground and they had to collect what they could reach. Older women taking part in the collection would also exploit this area, while the younger, fitter women would systematically harvest the targeted crop. During the monsoon the shell debris on the beach where the Anberra were collecting included many species washed up from deeper water, normally out of reach, but people collecting this debris tended to collect, cook and eat each species separately. Minor culinary matters also intervened in controlling the nature of the shellfish residue. A woman who had been collecting her quota of the target species (which took longer to cook) would add a few specimens of another fast-food species to be eaten while the main course was being prepared. Such minor details had a great deal of influence on the nature of the resulting archaeological record. Environmental archaeologists tend to interpret such organic residues in terms they can understand, such as environmental change or exhaustion of a particular resource, rather than in terms of behaviour, which is entirely reasonable since environmental change is a tangible and obvious thing, whereas the small nuances of human behaviour may only be inferred. Inference is not a scientific process. The example of the Anberra shows, however, that it may be behaviour rather than availability which conditions the food residues that accumulate on archaeological sites.

The further back in time that one goes the more difficult it becomes to sort out the complex factors which have produced these residues. Only by considering all factors which might have influenced the deposit, whether taphonomic, behavioural or environmental, will we be able to draw any conclusions about the how and why of hunting. Although handicapped by the limiting perspective imposed by the vast time gap separating our interpretations from the original accumulations, when dealing with palaeolithic sites, we do at least know something of the parameters which limited Stone Age society, including mobility, seasonality, territoriality and the like. When people begin to make a living in other ways, growing some of their food as well as catching it or picking it up, we run into a new series of problems, and it is these which are dealt with in the next chapter.

3
Eating

Nothing tells us more about a human community than what they ate. The acquisition of food is, and always has been, the major preoccupation of mankind, and the interpretation of food residues not only tells what people ate and why, but also how they lived. The expansion of interest in the type of information that such studies can provide is causally connected to the development and testing of new and better ways to extract the evidence for ancient diet.

The last ten years have seen innumerable technical advances in the laboratory which, alas, are seldom backed up by the integration of their results with the information obtained from artefacts and structures. It is now realised that different methods of approach need to be adopted not only for different types of sites but also for different preservation conditions. Many of the pioneering studies on the large-scale extraction of carbonised plant remains from archaeological sediments were carried out on the loose-textured sandy deposits of the Near East. Indeed, both the first froth-flotation device, called the Cambridge Froth Flotation Cell, and the method of separating off plant remains by water-sieving were initially used to investigate the origins of agriculture in that area. Any type of flotation depends on the principle that organic materials (e.g. carbonised seeds, literally turned to charcoal, retaining their original form after being heated in an atmosphere without oxygen) suspended in water are light, and that inorganic materials (the sandy components of a sediment) are relatively heavy and will sink. Simple flotation can be carried out by mixing sediment with water and pouring it through a sieve, when the lighter, carbonised material will be held in suspension and caught on the sieve and the heavier fraction can, with a little sleight of hand, be left behind in the bowl. But such methods are very amateurish and provide unrepresentative samples – the heavier fruit stones and many bones will be left behind. The development of froth-flotation was considered a great advance, and involved the use of a circular tank (often made from something like an oil drum) filled with water, paraffin and another chemical to produce a froth. Sediment was tipped in and air pumped into the mixture, resulting in the production of a froth which carried the light plant remains over the top of the tank into a series of collecting sieves which were then checked through (fig. 18). The residue was let out of the bottom of the tank into yet more sieves and checked over. The

18 A froth-flotation cell in operation. Light, carbonised material will be 'frothed' over the rim and caught in the nest of sieves. After each run is completed the sieves must be emptied, and the heavy residue let out into big sieves in the water trough before it, too, is sorted and bagged

method is quite slow and labour-intensive, also having the disadvantage of being unsuitable for heavy, clay-based soils which need to be disaggregated as otherwise it is impossible to separate out all the constituents.

There will always be deposits which present immense technical problems, like the plant foods and poisons from a late thirteenth- or early fourteenth-century storage pit in Chester. D. Gay Wilson's report is exceptional for its constructive but critical approach, and for the way in which the botanist concerned has realised the limitations of the results. Only 40g of material was available for analysis (all that was retrieved from the bottom of a 2m rock-cut cesspit) and most of that consisted of fruit stones. This is a classic case of non-random sampling; the attention of the excavator was called to the deposits because of the presence of the stones, but a sufficiently large sample was not taken to provide the botanist with statistically significant results. Moreover, the sample had been allowed to dry out. As a general rule waterlogged samples should be kept wet before separation of their organic constituents using wet-sieving or a flotation method. If allowed to dry out and then rehydrated, cracking and shrinkage would occur. Slow impregnation with a mixture of glycerine and alcohol is required, but the problem should never arise since waterlogged samples, properly packed (with a fungicide added and in stout bags or boxes) will last far better than dried ones. In this case the fruit stones were mainly from the sloe and bullace, which resembles a cherry-plum. It seems unlikely that this concentration of fruit stones is representative of the contents of the whole pit, although this could have been determined by sampling from other locations as well. In this case the pit was dug with a mechanical excavator with no environmental sampling programme, so that only the largest remains caught the eye. Other plant remains in the same pit were exceptionally fragmentary, so much so that grinding in a mortar during cooking preparation, or chewing and passing through the gut are suggested, confirming the interpretation of the pit as a cesspit. The fruit stones are, however, unlikely to have been swallowed, and these, together with sundry twigs and debris, presumably represent household garbage. Such a report serves as an illustration of many of the problems of dealing with plant material – notably preservation, extraction, identification and interpretation.

Waterlogged material can sometimes be exceptionally well preserved. Fig. 19 shows the original nineteenth-century illustration of the cereal and fruit remains retrieved from the neolithic sites often called Swiss 'lake villages', which were actually built at the side of lakes, allowing the dietary refuse to fall straight into the mud outside and become swiftly covered up by sediment under water. The resulting fruit, nuts and general rubbish is in almost as good a condition as when it was dropped nearly 6,000 years ago. Froth-flotation is only one of many devices, grouped under the heading of 'dirt-processing', which make the extraction of certain kinds of organic residues more effective. However, it would have been unsuitable for the Swiss lake village deposits, and is generally unsuited to waterlogged material, rather than carbonised remains. Froth-flotation is no use either for moss remains, pieces of wood or sorting out matted grasses and leaves, which are best extracted with combinations of wet-sieving and flotation using paraffin, which is also useful for sorting out insect remains (p. 106). Nor is it any use for the extraction of pollen or spores, which are far too small to be retained on any sieve and which must be sampled for separately. Only very small pollen samples (a few cubic centimetres) are required compared with the kilograms necessary for seed analysis, but their preparation involves a series of complicated laboratory processes involving separation of the pollen from the surrounding sediments using alternative treatments with different acids and alkalis, followed by mounting of the residue on a microscope slide and examination under high magnification to identify the type of pollen and relative numbers of plant species present. Such studies have been vital to our knowledge of vegetation history, especially, in an archaeological context, and to our understanding of the ways in which man has modified the landscape, introduced new plants, replaced others and altered the environment of an area to suit his own purposes.

The questions such activities pose are many and varied. How, for example, can we tell whether a plant actually grew on, or near, the location that we are

19 A pleasant nineteenth-century illustration of waterlogged food remains from the neolithic Swiss lakeside villages

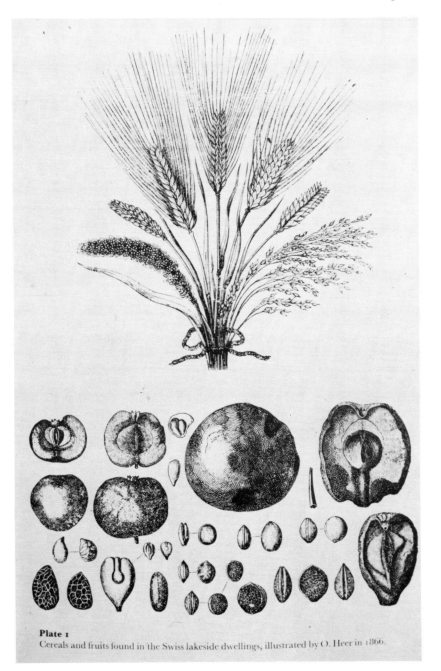

Plate 1
Cereals and fruits found in the Swiss lakeside dwellings, illustrated by O. Heer in 1866.

excavating? The evidence provided by environmental archaeology can sometimes be used to test out hypotheses about agriculture. For example, it has generally been thought, on the basis of very slender evidence, that the Romans grew vines and made wine in Britain. Historical sources are far from clear on the point but finds of grape seeds (for example the mineralised seeds obtained from a second-century context in the civilian settlement near the fort at Doncaster) may be more informative. The existence of mineralised seeds has only been realised quite recently, and earlier excavations might well have failed to realise their presence. Environmental archaeologists are now stressing the fact that isolated finds of a species from a single context may be easily misinterpreted and large samples of material should be examined, using proper, statistically calculated sampling procedures. Without such measures it is impossible, returning to the case of grapes, to distinguish the seeds of imported from home-grown varieties of grape, nor can one comment on the importance of grapes in the diet. Grape seeds alone do not constitute proof that grapes were grown – but this could be obtained by getting corroborative evidence in the form of pollen analysis from buried surfaces in Romano-British rural sites and villas. There are a number of finds of grape skins, seeds and debris from a pit in Gloucester, excavated in the nineteenth century, but few references to finds of vine stems or wood, probably since comparatively little attention has been paid to Romano-British rural sites since the upsurge of interest in environmental archaeology in the 1970s. In order to prove vine-growing, preserved wood remains or leaves are essential, but here we meet a snag since exceptionally good preservation conditions are required for their survival, unlike pollen or grape seeds which are much tougher and survive in a far wider range of burial conditions. The grape seeds found may have come from imported raisins, and although many such finds are reported it is difficult to say precisely what they mean. The vine is, anyway, near the northern limit of its geographical range in Britain and could probably have only flourished in small walled gardens, rather than the open-plan French vineyards. However, the discovery of some vine wood at the Boxmoor Roman villa, taken together with the evidence from Gloucester, would seem to suggest that vine-growing was a possibility, especially since that area became predominant in medieval wine production and there seems to be a strong correlation between the distribution of medieval vineyards and the main regions of Roman civilian settlements.

The problem of interpreting vine seeds in many ways epitomises some of the difficulties encountered by those who try to reconstruct diet. Fig seeds, for example, were recovered from the Roman town of Silchester yet the fig species represented come from varieties which cannot be grown in this country and are therefore exotic imports. The Romans imported many different types of exotic species such as the lentil, olive and cucumber which often figure prominently in their refuse deposits. At St Thomas Street in Southwark all these occurred in a pit together with all sorts of other fruits such as mulberry, blackberry, raspberry, sloe, plum, cherry, coriander, dill,

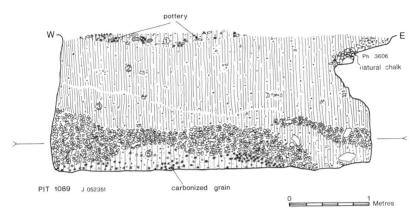

pottery

W

E

Ph 3606
natural chalk

PIT 1089   J 052351   carbonized grain

0   1 Metres

20 Deposits of charred grain, like this example from an eroded chalk-cut storage pit from the Iron Age hillfort at Danebury, Hants, can not only produce information about crops being cultivated but also about the function of archaeological features

carraway and elderberry, which presumably represent the range of fruits and vegetables available to a fraction of the population of Roman London at one small segment of time. But how does one work out from lists such as these the species which actually dominated? At Doncaster a pit was found which contained vast quantities of apple seeds, representing between 150 and 300 apples together with some other fruits. Was this because apples were the favourite fruit of the inhabitants, do they represent the debris of cider-making, or are they merely the remains of rotten fruit that had been thrown away?

New advances are constantly being made in the recognition and identification of the remains of ancient diet. As early as 1969 Hans Helbaek had noted the presence of seeds which had been preserved not by carbonisation or waterlogging but by mineralisation (replacement of the organic fraction of the seeds by calcium or gypsum salts) and ten years later Frank Green identified phosphate-mineralised seeds. These are generally a honey-brown in colour and quite difficult to recognise, but they are important for two reasons; firstly, they are frequently quite well-preserved in ordinary unwaterlogged soils, and secondly, they are most common in faecal deposits, such as the cesspits or garderobe pits described below (p. 109), as a result of passing through the human digestive tract. Mineralised seeds thus represent direct evidence of diet, but (inevitably) such evidence is not unbiased as only certain varieties of seeds can survive the human digestive processes intact. The commonest mineralised seeds to be retrieved are cereal grains (fig. 20), especially oats, wheat and barley, together with fruit pips and stones, the remains of plums, cherries, figs, and different berries, an example being the Roman grape pips, described above. Careful analysis of deposits rich in mineralised seeds can give some idea of the constituents of an ancient diet, but they must be retrieved by laborious hand picking since they are comparatively heavy and cannot be 'floated' away from their matrix. The 'seed machines' already mentioned have become familiar, in slightly different guises, on many archaeolgical excavations but have quite restricted applications. If the archaeological deposit is waterlogged (as it might be at the bottom of a well, for example) it is very difficult to separate the carbonised seeds from a mass of soggy waterlogged plant fibres. Botanists are constantly debating the mesh size of sieves which must be used in flotation devices, with some general agreement now being reached on 1mm and 0.5mm mesh. Such sieves will catch small animal bones and many plant remains but a certain fraction of the latter will inevitably be lost, such as the tiny weed seeds or fragments of chaff. However, whatever method is used, great care in sampling must be taken, as it is necessary to take both 'random' samples during an excavation, in order to assess what is known as 'background' flora, and samples from specific contexts like storage pits, hearths or floor levels. The best impression of food plants can undoubtedly be obtained from rubbish contexts, like cesspits, or from coprolite (faeces) which also contains direct evidence of diet but is only rarely preserved, except where conditions are very dry.

A great deal of work on coprolite has been done from the palaeoindian sites of the southern part of America, where not only the remains of food plants but also of insects including grasshoppers and locusts which were eaten in large quantities have been recovered, accompanied by the evidence for a wide variety of parasitic diseases including various gut parasites and lice. However, the occurrence of such material is exceptional and generally the archaeologist is forced to rely on the systematic extraction of seeds and other plant remains from the sediments on his site. Such studies are quite expensive – six years ago Helen Keeley of the Ancient Monuments Laboratory in London estimated that the processing of one sample for its macroscopic organic remains could cost £100 and take one to three weeks for each category of organic material (bones, seeds, molluscan remains etc.). This figure includes the expensive specialist time required for complex identifications, but would certainly be very much higher in the present day. Excavation budgets are shrinking as archaeological techniques expand, and there is a marked dichotomy in the subject between those excavators (a growing breed) who consider that to dig and publish a site without a full sampling programme for all the organic material is unjustifiable and means the job is only being half done, and those who consider that the primary job of the archaeologist is to extract objects and the remains of structures from the ground, organic materials being properly left to 'scientists'. Expense is naturally a consideration and so is time – with more people requiring specialist assistance, an environmentalist who works, let us say, on the identification of seeds, may have a 'waiting list' of several years' work which extends the (often considerable) amount of time that elapses beween the excavation and the appearance of the report. And how do you publish all this specialised biological information when publication itself is so expensive? One solution is to include only the major facts necessary to the interpretation of the site within the main text, and to consign the bulk of the reports, which may consist of extensive data tables, to microfiche sheets slotted into a pocket at the back of the article. This solution, recommended at present by the Council for British Archaeology as a cost-saving device, is only an intermediate stage and will undoubtedly be replaced by fully-computerised data storage and publication of all aspects of the site bioarchaeology within a few years. But how this solves the problem of processing sheer quantities of samples by relatively few people no one yet knows. Perhaps we should all stop excavating?

Anyway, moving aside from technical and professional problems for a moment, let us consider just what we know about human dietary preferences. We have already considered the gradual evolution from a scavenging to a hunting and foraging way of life, with the beginnings of animal-management at the end of the palaeolithic. Until this stage human communities were still relatively thinly spread over the globe, each busy adapting to the problems posed by their particular set of environmental and cultural conditions. It is with the advent of domestication, settled farming and all the concomitant social changes that this brought, that a great change takes place; not overnight but over hundreds and sometimes thousands of years, between the end of the mesolithic, where small highly-mobile communities are occupying selected territories and endeavouring to make a living by a constant battle against nature, to the present day where nature hardly exists anymore, and man has achieved dominance over the entire planet. Since such a dramatic event happened in so short a time – less than 10,000 years since the invention of farming, compared with billions of years of evolution beforehand – we are forced to seach for a reason, and the key must lie in the changes in social organisation and behaviour that are intimately connected with the development of agriculture, since it is agriculture – the domestication of crops and animals – which has enabled man to control and tame so large a part of the world and expand his population to such a great extent.

It is difficult to overestimate the significance of these developments which, in the early days of archaeology, were thought sufficiently important to merit the term 'Neolithic Revolution', comparable, say, with the Industrial Revolution. But the term 'revolution' implies some sudden change, and this was certainly not the case. With each passing year we are discovering that the origins of agriculture must be sought much further back in time than had previously been imagined, and that human communities fresh from the Ice Age began to experiment and innovate with their food supply. The remains of food are, unfortunately, perishable, so supplementary evidence of diet (the presence of flint sickles, or grinding wheels) may become important, although these do not tell us exactly what wild plants were being harvested, or whether these plants were being modified (bred, domesticated) in any way. For this we need the remains of the plants and animals themselves, either in the form of bones (for the latter) or, most commonly, of seeds (for the former). Analysis of the origins of food production used to concentrate on the Middle East, the so-called 'Fertile Crescent' extending from Egypt to Mesopotamia, under the mistaken impression that it was here, and only here, that agriculture began (fig. 21). However, we now know that although the Middle East was undoubtedly the cradle of agriculture (sheep/goats were domesticated here by 9000 BC and primitive wheat and barley was being grown a couple of millenia later) in south-east Asia food plants, including peas and beans, had been domesticated by 7000 BC and in Mexico, by 6000 BC, the Indians of the Andes were growing different varieties of beans. By 3000 BC rice was being grown in China and the palaeoindian agriculturalists of Mexico had developed, quite independently, a system based on the cultivation of squash and beans replaced, around 3000 BC, by corn growing.

These separate centres of innovation show that agriculture was one further step in human development which could, and did, take place independently in many different areas. No doubt some still remain to be located. The reason for the initial concentration of interest in the Middle East was partly a historical one (it was, after all, a traditional focus for archaeological activity). It was also where the wild wheat grew of its own accord, permitting a gradual transition from hunter-gatherer societies to groups which were partly dependent on wild crops, staying, perhaps, in one area where the grain was prolific. From this stage it was only a small step to plant some of the grains and grow them, although the diet of the communities was not transformed overnight and always included wild plants as well as cultivated ones, and wild animals as well as domesticates. This is true right up to the present day, where our sophisticated Western diet still includes a 'wild' component, but often as luxury foods. So how do we know when these first steps were taken? The answer lies in the careful and systematic analysis of food remains, especially seeds. After sampling the archaeological sediments and extracting the material, the botanist must identify each seed and assign it to a species; wild and domesticated cereals look very different and even the grains can be told apart. An expert can not only distinguish wild from cultivated crops, but also comment on the stage of domestication that had been reached. Two varieties of wheat grow wild in the Middle East, wild eincorn (*Triticum boeticum*) and wild emmer (*Triticum diccoides*). These were nutritious but had a grave disadvantage to primitive farmers; the seed-bearing ear of corn would shatter as soon as it was ripe making it difficult to harvest the crop with primitive sickles (fig. 22). Man therefore selected the grains with the toughest spikes which did not disintegrate on harvesting and, by this discrimination, produced a strain of domesticated wheat by 7000 BC.

At first, wild and domesticated cereals both formed part of the farmer's diet, but careful breeding of resistant strains (with larger seeds) ensured the supremacy of the cultivated variety (fig. 23). Wheat and barley did not, however, form the sole diet of these early farmers who began to grow chick-peas, lentils and beans around the same time, and gradually expanded their capabilities to the cultivation of fruits (figs, apricots) nuts (walnut, almond and pistachio) and, a little later, the olive and grape. In America potatoes, an alternative food staple, were grown by 2000 BC, again with the beans which were a valuable source of protein, although corn had been cultivated in rich agricultural lands of Mexico by 5500 BC, and all sorts of minor crops (chillies and the cocoa bean) made up quite a different agricultural basis. Corn in Mexico, millet and soya beans in China, potatoes in the Andes – all different staple foods for farmers and all domesticated at different times. Bioarchaeologists are working on many problems associated with these developments, for example in the project initiated by Richard McNeish to trace the origins and development of corn-growing in Mexico. This project undertook the excavation of a series of cave sites and the gradual reconstruction of the processes by which corn had been domesticated over nearly 5,000 years in the Tehuacan Valley in Southern Mexico. Another project working in caves in the High Andes turned up the remains of large and clearly domesticated beans dating to 5600 BC, and so it goes on.

The social changes which accompanied this alteration in human diet were dramatic and far-reaching. The first farming villages were the first links in a chain which led gradually towards urbanisation and civilisation, and to a world where the majority of the population lived away from the land and gained its food by bartering some sort of service, which, unless we happen to be farmers, is exactly what we do today. But food plants were not the only things to be subject to the process of domestication; animals were just as important, and with animals the whole process started earlier, arguably as early as the last stages of the palaeolithic. The origins of animal domestication certainly lie in the herding practices of the last great hunting bands, who followed the annual movement of a reindeer group or selectively culled certain members of an animal community at specific times of the year. But domestication of animals means far more than that, it means altering the actual shape and characteristics of the animal in some way to make it more suitable for the purpose for which it was intended. Not all animals can be domesticated, and not all are domesticated for the same reason. Some, such as the elephant or camel, were bred for transport purposes, while others were kept for different reasons, as pets, for hunting (as in the case of birds of prey) or for ritual reasons. Not all animals were domesticated to equal extents and there is a 'sliding-scale' produced by the bioarchaeologist Don Brothwell to describe this phenomenon, starting with a very tenuous association between man and animal (such as the initial taming of dogs to aid in hunting) and ending in the complete dependence of the animal species on man, which we see today in factory-farming methods. There is rather a pathetic little story about the hazards presented by wild dogs in Egypt, quoted in a recent book by the Egyptologist A.-P. Leca, who translates from a papyrus written by an official marooned in a frontier post:

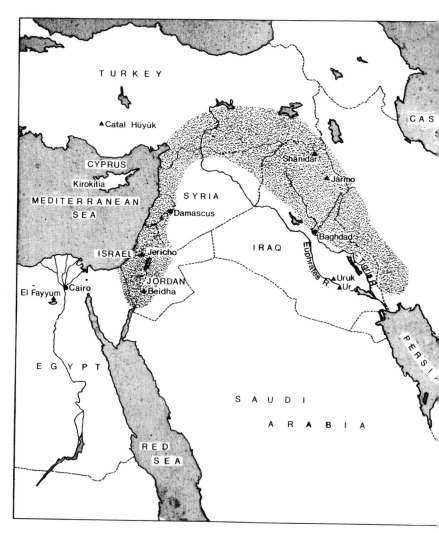

21 The 'Fertile Crescent', stretching
from Egypt to Mesopotamia, where
the earliest animal domestication took
place. Triangles mark important sites,
mentioned in the text

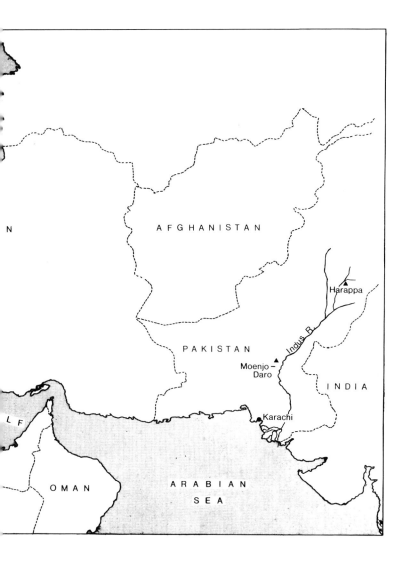

22 In order to harvest cereals with a flint-bladed sickle, grasp a handful of stalks firmly and then saw them through. One of the reasons for domesticating such plants was to produce varieties whose grains still stayed in the ears throughout this operation

> If ever I open a pot of beer and take it outside to drink, two hundred big dogs and three hundred wolf-dogs appear, five hundred in all. Every day they are in front of the door, every time I go out, because of the smell from the pot when it is opened. What would happen to me if I did not have here the young wolf-dog belonging to Nahiho the royal scribe? He is the only one to save me from them whenever I go out, and he guides me along the way.

A hard life when you can't enjoy a pint of beer in peace, but illustrative of the importance that Man's Best Friend played, even from early times.

Distinguishing a wild from a domestic animal is done by essentially the same means as that already described for plants; it is necessary to recover the remains (generally bones), usually via some flotation device, assign them to a particular part of the body, then to a species, and eventually characterise the animals which composed part of the fauna from a site, distinguishing wild from domestic forms. This sounds a lot easier than it is, and 'archaeozoology', the oldest and largest branch of bioarchaeology, produces hundreds of papers annually devoted to problems of distinguishing domestic animals. It is generally agreed that 22 different animal species were domesticated during the period between 8500 BC (when Middle Eastern farmers first herded sheep/goats) and 1000 BC, including everything from guinea-pigs in Peru to the more commonly studied bones of pigs, sheep, goats and cattle which have

23 The spike of wild emmer wheat on the left has smaller, slimmer grains than the domesticated variety on the right

been much studied. At the moment the first domestication of sheep seems to date to around 8500 BC at the site of Zawi Chemi Shanidar in the Zagros mountains of Northern Iraq, (fig. 21), and of cattle to 6500 BC (in Greece and Turkey). It is hardly surprising that the domestication of sheep and goats should have begun so early and in the Middle East, since it is there that their wild prototypes lived and were hunted for thousands of years earlier. In the very early stage of domestication it is hard for the zoologist to distinguish between the bones of sheep and goat (hence the invention of that unique archaeological hybrid the 'sheep-goat'), nor is it easy to say whether wild or domestic forms are represented. It is necessary to compare the bones with existent wild species, although there is now always doubt about how 'wild' these still are. It is possible to see gradual changes; the horn cores of goats, for example, change in cross-section from an almond shape (in wild forms) to a kidney shape in domestic varieties. Sheep horn cores change as well, cattle were bred from the now extinct wild auroch (wild ox) to the gentle tame cows of the present day, and virtually every species of potential domestic importance, from alpaca (domesticated for its wool) to chickens (domesticated in India around 2000 BC), was gradually adapted to human needs.

Not all domestic animals serve the same purpose in different areas: some breeds of sheep, for example, are raised for wool and others are raised for meat. In the Gobi Desert camels are used to pull the carts on which are the

24 Cakes of dried yoghurt (*aroug*) made from camel's milk and spread out to dry on the roof of a white felt *ger*, Outer Mongolia

entire possessions of a Mongol family, including the collapsed white, round, felt tent (*ger*, or *yurt* in Russian) and all their personal belongings (fig. 50). They are the two-humped Bactrian variety which, as well as acting as beasts of burden provide meat, milk, and hair for ropes and textile manufacture. Unlike the single-humped camel of North Africa, they are never ridden and their milk, when fermented and dried into hard pungent cakes, makes the solid yoghurt called *aroug* (fig. 24) which may, when accompanied by *ayraq* (*kumiss*), a drink made from fermented mare's milk, provide the complete basis of nourishment over the winter or when meat is scarce. These Mongols, like the old farmers shown milking their prize mares in fig. 25, are pastoral nomads, traditionally reliant on their herds for everything from food and drink to transport and shelter. In Mongolia the first records of such a way of life date to the fourth century BC, although wandering nomadism is now being reduced by government collectivisation into large state production units. In the more remote areas of the country, however, modern technology and political changes have made little impact on this essentially medieval lifestyle. The archaeological record suggests that the Scythian nomads, whose most spectacular remains are the graves at Pazyryk (p. 136), lived in a very similar fashion, hardly surprising as the self-reliant nomadic lifestyle is entirely suitable for life on the steppes or desert fringes. Scythians, like the modern Mongols, spent hours in the saddle, were proud of their horse-breeding and archery skills, and also made *kumiss* in the traditional way; the goatskins hanging in a modern *ger* on the fringes of the Gobi (fig. 26) would

25 Milking mares, Mongolia

have been a familiar site in the area 2,500 years ago. The folding trellis-work of a *ger* framework is portrayed as a scratched engraving on a stone marking an eighth-century AD grave (fig. 27), now often covered by white canvas if the family is wealthy, but with the traditional warm layers of felt underneath.

Traditional Mongol diet, consisting of meat and milk products, is particularly well adapted to a nomadic lifestyle, but human dietary preferences may be dictated by many things – religious needs, for example, or social status, as well as sheer availability. The so-called 'bog burials' from Denmark, now numbering over a hundred individuals in different stages of preservation, owe their remarkable survival to the damp, anaerobic environment which received their bodies and to the 'tanning' effect of the peaty waters. The bodies, dating from the Iron Age to the medieval period, have been found largely as a result of large-scale post-war peat-cutting in the area, and their cause of death is as variable as their preservation. The calm face of Tollund man (fig. 28), despite the rope round his neck, has caught many people's imagination, and he was one of the two burials whose stomach contents were investigated by Hans Helbaek, back in the early days of 'palaeoethnobotany', as it is now called. It was, not unreasonably, hoped that by actually working on the preserved remains of food, still, so to speak, *in situ*, first-hand evidence of Iron Age diet could be obtained, but, as we shall see, the matter did not prove to be that simple. Helbaek, working over 30 years ago, examined the stomach content of both the Tollund and Graubelle men, both dating from the Iron Age, and found not only large quantities of preserved plant remains, some even producing information on ancient crop diseases, but also intestinal parasites. The constituents of these presumably

26 Goatskins filled with *ayraq* (*kumiss*) in the process of fermentation. Note the trellis-work wall of the *ger* behind them

'last meals' were, however, extremely curious in the quantity and variety of plants represented – far more than one would expect from an everyday Iron Age diet. In the case of Graubelle man, for example, 66 species of seed and grain were recovered, all but 11 being wild. Why eat so many wild grasses? Archaeologists think that these burials are possibly ritual sacrifices and that the meals, eaten apparently less than 24 hours before death, were a hotchpotch of vegetable matter, unrepresentative of everyday diet and probably taken to ensure continued crop and animal fertility as part of a human sacrifice.

Helbaek commented on the numerous problems, not only in interpretation, presented by the material. It was (inevitably) in different degrees of disintegration, so it was difficult to calculate the relative proportions of the crops represented. The Graubelle remains, rather better preserved than Tollund, were certainly dominated by wheat and rye, complete with the crop disease ergot of rye, caused by a mould (*Claviceps purpurea*) which is referred to in classical sources. In addition to these cereals, seeds of 11 weed and wild grass species also occurred, from plants with very different habitat requirements. No fruits or berries, which would give some evidence of the season at which the burials (sacrifices?) had been made, were recovered. Weed seeds did, it seems, form part of the general diet of Danish Iron Age men, but this strange mixture almost certainly did not. In addition to the cereals and weeds large quantities of linseed remains occurred – the plant

27 Eighth-century grave marker, Gobi Desert, showing the scratched design of a *ger*

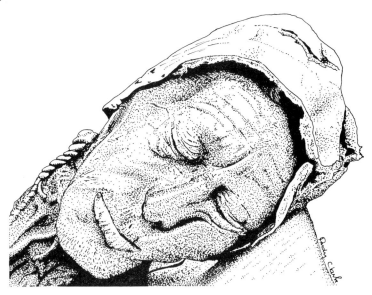

28 Tollund man, preserved by waterlogging and partly tanned by peaty waters, still looks amazingly serene

having been utilised mainly for its oil – and the protein component of the mixture came from piglet, although it was less important than the plant. This ghastly mixture was reconstructed on television as a splendid piece of early experimental archaeology which starred the late great Sir Mortimer Wheeler. The resulting mixture, apparently an unpleasing yellow colour with splodges of purple, was nobly sampled in full view of an eager (and sadistic) audience but pronounced to taste better than it looked! The identification of these burials as having 'ritual' significance (a term from which modern archaeologists shrink as it has so often been used as a cover-all for behavioural patterns which they are unable to interpret) does, of course, rest on more than stomach-content analyses, but these curious last meals do seem to provide supporting evidence.

There will always be such conundrums in the archaeological records, such as the first appearance of new and exotic foods – grown at home or imported via some newly-opened trade route? In disentangling the dietary record the archaeologist has to deal with factors which may not be documented at all; for example, the different foods eaten by people at different levels in the social scale. People do not easily change their way of life. In 1973 the anthropologist Colin Turnbull produced a controversial book about the Ik, a tribe of nomad hunters who were driven from their hunting grounds in the barren mountains of eastern Uganda and told to take up farming, although they had no knowledge of farming techniques and had been deposited in a land where there was little or no rain. The results were disastrous; within 50 years all the social conventions of the tribe had vanished because of their inability to change their lifestyle. The Ik did not, however, resort to cannibalism although there are many examples in the historical and archaeological record of this distasteful practice. It has been claimed that the practice began as early as the middle palaeolithic and that neanderthals were cannibals, although if this is so (and the bone evidence is now much disputed, p. 31) they seem likely to have practised very selective eating of parts of other human beings, perhaps only the brain, for ritual rather than nourishing reasons. The most quoted example is the neanderthal skull from the cave of Monte Circeo, near Rome (fig. 29) which had apparently been broken for extraction of the brain. Although this type of mutilation may be seen today in Melanesian tribes who still continue this practice, some people have suggested that the skull has merely been gnawed by carnivores. Since it was found within a ring of stones and had clearly originally been positioned on a short stake, brain eating seems more likely. Such selective cannibalism is quite common in hunter-gatherer societies and there is much anthropological evidence for it.

Eating humans as a simple dietary preference is not, however, well evidenced archaeologically as during the palaeolithic it would generally have been unnecessary (people are quite difficult to hunt and butcher and don't provide much meat in return for the effort, especially in comparison with the large game animals) and in later periods more complex social

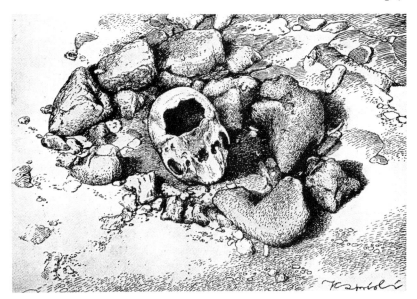

29 Upturned Neanderthal skull from the cave of Monte Circeo, near Rome. The base was probably mutilated for the extraction of the brain, a custom still practised today in Melanesia

structures would have made the practice unlikely. Cannibalism for preference (as opposed to reasons associated with ritual, religion or war) probably survives into the present day and was described in great detail by Victorians who ventured into Central Africa during the days of apocryphal missionary-boiling. In the Congo the Rev. Holman Bentley, who spent 20 years in the region, quoted one local as saying 'You white men consider pork to be the tastiest of meat, but pork is not to be compared with human flesh. You eat fowls and goats, and we eat men; why not? What is the difference?' Difficult to answer, but under Belgian colonial administration cannibalism became much rarer, although in 1956 H.C. Engert noted that it was still extensively practised. One presumes that lack of archaeological evidence must therefore be for reasons of dietary preference, rather than scruples.

This diversion into exotic dietary preferences may seem irrelevant but it does show that the archaeological evidence for human diet, at any period, is likely to be subject to a whole series of different biasing factors, not all of which may be obvious. Fig. 30 shows the distribution of walnut shells found at different levels during the excavation of the medieval town of Novgorod, described in more detail below (p. 100). Novgorod, situated in the coniferous forests of northern Russia, does not at present possess a climate favourable for the growing of walnuts yet the inhabitants were clearly enjoying this delicacy from before 1000 AD. The distribution of walnut shells shows them to be most

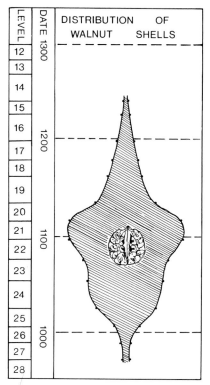

LEVEL	DATE	DISTRIBUTION OF WALNUT SHELLS
12	1300	
13		
14		
15		
16		
17	1200	
18		
19		
20		
21	1100	
22		
23		
24		
25		
26	1000	
27		
28		

30 Walnuts were imported to Novgorod from the Mediterranean but are not present in all archaeological layers.

common between 1000 and 1200 AD (archaeological layers 25–16) and tailing off dramatically after layer 15. What could be the reason? Several interpretations are possible. Firstly, we could suggest that the climate of the area in the early medieval period was different from the present day; perhaps there was a short period of warmer temperatures which permitted walnut-growing. But there is no supporting evidence of walnut wood, leaves or pollen, suggesting that just the nuts were imported. Perhaps the eating of walnuts was merely a fashion which became outmoded after 1200? Perhaps the archaeological levels after 1200 did not preserve walnuts in the same way as earlier strata, imparting a bias to the evidence? The actual explanation is far simpler; walnuts grow in warm Mediterranean climates and were imported from the south; the graph merely illustrates the intensity of these southern trade routes, which fluctuated at various periods. In the eleventh century, Russian trade with the south was at a maximum but it gradually tailed off, until interrupted by the Mongol incursions. These were the last of a wave of pastoral nomads who had swept out of their homes on the Central

Asian steppes from the eighth century onwards. About 1200 AD the unification of the Mongols under Temujin (Genghis Khan) established an empire from China to northern Europe; although never reaching as far as Novgorod their destruction of southern Russia in 1240 cut off trade connections with the Byzantine world, and the inhabitants of Novgorod had to go without their walnuts, as well as their box-tree wood, sponges, Persian pottery, exotic glassware and almonds. Even when the trade routes with the south had been flourishing it is unlikely that all members of society (not quite as egalitarian then as now) would have, in any case, been able to develop a partiality for walnuts, which, as imported goods, must always have been rather expensive.

We can take another example nearer home – during the Tudor period the establishment of trade routes between England and America resulted in the introduction of a number of new, exotic foods into England (potatoes, tropical fruits and spices, turkey) but oranges did not appear on the tables of any but the very rich. Less than 100 years ago the tomato was still regarded by many conservative Englishmen as poisonous, and it is only within the last 20 years that the decreasing cost of foreign holidays, accustoming the English traveller to foreign foods, combined with ease of transport, has resulted in the inclusion of Mediterranean vegetables such as peppers, courgettes, aubergines and garlic in English kitchen waste. How will these dietary remains be interpreted by the bioarchaeologists of the future? The position is additionally complicated by the domestic deep-freeze, which enables us to eat any fruit and vegetable at any time of the year, removing all traces of seasonality from our dietary residues. At least they will have the benefits of documentary records to accompany their studies, while we, when studying the prehistoric record, must rely largely upon inference.

It is much easier to interpret the precise components of an ancient diet if some corroborative information is present. This may be done at various scales, from the individual site to really large-scale reconstructions such as sorting out the food requirements and preferences of the Roman army. A great deal of documentary evidence is available, for example from the historian Josephus, or the scenes on Trajan's Column, but the sheer volume of food required by such an enormous military machine, and the problems of supplying it, are difficult to overestimate. Tacitus says that every Roman fort in Britain contained enough supplies to last its garrison for a year. This can be used to work out precise details – each Roman soldier received three pounds of corn per day meaning that at certain times during the Roman occupation over 10,000 tons of grain would have been required in Britain to feed the army alone. We can use historical sources to tell us about the individual food preferences of emperors or soldiers, and even about individual dietary awareness (in Petronius's *Satyricon* Habinnas says, when attending Trimalchio's banquet, based on Nero's legendary feasts, that he prefers brown bread to white because it was nourishing and prevents constipation). Detailed information is not, however, available about the diet of the army

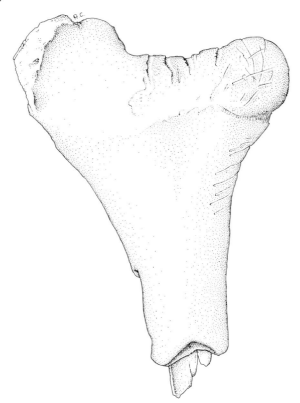

31 Cut marks on the top of an ox
femur, the result of Roman army cuisine

and for many years it was assumed that the soldiers' diet did not include
meat. This has now been contradicted by an analysis of the animal bone
assemblages from Roman sites in Britain and Germany. It would seem that
the soldiers had plenty of meat (bought from locals, obtained by hunting or as
the result of ritual sacrifices), mostly the domesticated ox, with some sheep, a
few goats and a little pork. Analysis also produced information on the precise
joints eaten – many of the bones came from immature animals, suggesting
that the troops ate beef, veal, mutton, lamb, pork and sucking-pig. Fig. 31
shows the butchery marks which remain on a cattle femur from one of these
sites. Military equipment included army-issue boiling pans and spits and the
soldiers clearly had a fondness for stew since many of the beef bones had been
split down the middle to obtain the marrow, presumably to add to the pot.
Bones from all parts of the carcasses were present, suggesting that the entire
animal (rather than selected joints) had been eaten, and by-products such as
cheese were also produced, as indicated by cheese-squeezers from military

sites. Not all the bones came from domestic animals; some were hunted, a way of combining sport with the addition of fresh meat to the diet. Red and roe deer, elk, wild boar and hare were hunted for meat and presumably fox, wolf, badger, bear and otter contributed sport and fur. Roman soldiers also liked shellfish and fish. At the legionary fortress of Vindonissa fish-bones and a fish-hook were found, and other sites located strategically near the sea (such as Richborough) or a river (Valkenburg on the Rhine) produced fish remains.

The reason that comparatively little work has been done on fish remains is a simple one – fish-bones are small, easily overlooked in a section, and generally recoverable only by some laborious wet-sieving method. In addition, fish-bones are often fragile and, being so small, may be difficult to identify. On most sites fish-bones appear in low concentrations, but, in addition to the bones (jaws and vertebrae tend to survive best) there is the possibility of recovering earstones (otoliths) which may often be identified to species, and fish scales. Both these categories of material grow annual rings which may aid not only in establishing the size of the fish (and thus the weight of meat that it represents) but also the season of the year at which it was caught, which may give a clue to when the site was occupied. Even a large fish leaves quite a small weight of bone compared, let us say, with a mammal, which means that great care must be taken in sieving and extraction of bone if a full set of data is to be obtained. Andrew Jones, working at the site of Fuller's Hill, Great Yarmouth in East Anglia, estimated that he had processed several tons of well-stratified sandy deposits using a 1mm sieve mesh to extract a mere 8kg of fish-bones and scales. Since the site was a fishing port the effort, although considerable, was clearly worthwhile and it does illustrate the comparative scarcity of bioarchaeological remains in cultural strata, and the great efforts that must be made to extract them.

It is rare for any people to gain their entire protein source from fish, which usually form part of a mixed economy. However, the type of fish whose remains appear in a deposit is dependent upon a number of different factors, including the location of the site (whether or not, for example, its inhabitants could have access to river or lake species), the technology of its inhabitants (did they have the ability to carry out deep-sea fishing or the necessary tackle for particular species?) as well as dietary preferences and other cultural factors. Fish remains can therefore produce information about past fishing activities, not merely about diet. The depth range of a species affects the fishing method chosen, for example, and in the exploitation of marine fish one needs to take into account questions such as their seasonal migrations, or behaviour in shoals. Prehistoric fish remains often form part of midden deposits, where it is necessary to calculate the relative meat weights represented by the fish, molluscs and birds which accompany them. Andrew Jones, working on Saxon and medieval deposits from Ipswich, again in East Anglia, was able, as a result of a well-thought out sampling strategy and very careful sieving procedures, to suggest that one feature of the fish remains, namely the number of herring-bones, changed over the period whose deposits were being examined. Far more herring-bones were being incorporated into rubbish pits between the end of the Middle Saxon period and the beginning of the Saxo-Norman occupation than had been seen before, but this was not true for other fish which would have also been eaten during this period. So why a sudden increase in herring-bone at this time? Jones suggested that two explanations were possible, a technological one (perhaps the introduction of a drift net) to increase the efficiency of the herring fishermen, or else an environmental one, notably a change in the distribution of herring in the North Sea which brought them nearer to the fishing grounds which were being worked from Ipswich. Either explanation is possible, and the case study illustrates the many difficulties inherent in bioarchaeological explanations where so many factors remain unknown.

Eating fish was not always, apparently, a good idea. R.W. Davies, in a classic article on Roman military diet, quotes a rather pathetic letter written in the early second century by one Terentianus, a legionary stationed at Alexandria, who failed to turn up for a meeting with his father because:

> ... it was at that time that so violent and dreadful an attack of fish poisoning made me ill, and for five days I was unable to drop you a line, not to speak of going to meet you. Not one of us was even able to leave the camp gate.

The culprit seems to have been a fish known only by its Latin name, *maeotes*, which is described by the Roman writer Athenaeus as delicious, but which we are unable to identify further. Taking together the evidence provided by papyri, epigraphy and literary references together with the 'windows' on military diet provided by bioarchaeological investigation of selected contexts, a good picture of the Roman military diet can be obtained, but it is selective and biased in favour of those species which happen to survive, or whose presence is recorded. However, it is impossible completely to eliminate bias since the archaeological record is very selective, and made the more so by poor excavation and sampling techniques. The bioarchaeologist interested in the reconstruction of ancient diet must do the best he can with evidence that will always be incomplete, but technical advances (in sampling, in the laboratory, and in the statistical processing of results) mean that at last it is possible for us to gain at least some idea of ancient diet, even though the preserved evidence is patchy and difficult to interpret. After all, if we 'are what we eat' then we need to understand early diet before we can come to grips with understanding early culture.

4
Ailing

The study of plant diseases in antiquity is a relatively new one for the archaeologist, stimulated by developments in microbiology, and by the realisation that the large-scale crop diseases now familiar to us made their first appearance soon after the development of farming. In the absence of modern pesticides, many seem likely to have had catastrophic effects on community life, including the occasional large-scale famine. An uncontrollable epidemic disease which struck at some carbohydrate or protein-rich food staple, especially cereals, would inevitably have created hardship, if not actual famine. Indeed, this occurred quite recently with the Irish potato famine of 1845–9, caused by the fungus *Phytophthora infestans*, probably introduced into Ireland with potatoes from Central or South America, which spread at the incredible rate of 80km per week. This rapid dispersal, combined with a total lack of knowledge about the cause or prevention of the disease resulted in a reduction of the population of Ireland from over eight million (three or four of whom relied on the potato as a major food staple) to less than six million, with many families being forced to emigrate and the initiation of major social and demographic changes. It is inevitable that catastrophes of similar magnitude occurred in earlier times, but the chances of detecting them are slight. Classical writers describe the effects of plant disease, but such information is not quantitative, and it is often impossible to identify the organism concerned.

There are a few examples of diseased plants from archaeological contexts, although as yet no large-scale systematic reconstruction of patterns of plant disease is possible. Analysis of the well-preserved Iron Age corpses of the Bog people from Denmark (fig. 28) produced quite a lot of evidence for crop diseases, particularly those caused by fungi such as the smut *Ustilago* spp. which attack cereals, and other food-spoiling moulds such as ergot of rye (*Claviceps purpurea*) which, if eaten in large quantities, will produce gangrene and death. The stomach contents of the Tollund and Grauballe men, when analysed by the botanist Hans Helbaek, produced samples of cereal grains infested with this disease, which attacks many wild grasses as well as cultivated grains but is especially frequent on rye. It is usually harvested with the grain and can thus contaminate both human and animal foodstuffs. It was clearly a common disease in prehistoric times but the first written descriptions of its effect are much later, dating from 857 AD when the village of

Kanten on the Lower Rhine suffered a plague which conforms to the descriptions of ergot poisoning. A similar outbreak occurred in Paris in 945 AD and plagues of 'ergotism' or 'St Anthony's Fire' (so called because one of the major symptoms is inflammation of the limbs) as a result of infected grains were quite common in early medieval Europe, reaching a peak in the eleventh and twelfth centuries. It decreased in intensity from the eighteenth century onwards, as a result of the increasing popularity of wheat over rye, and later, of potatoes as a food staple.

Such changes in agricultural practice and varying popularity of different foods are very difficult to detect in the archaeological record which is inevitably incomplete and, even if such a change is noted, the cause may be wrongly assigned. The apparently dramatic decline in finds of walnut shells (p. 72) in medieval Novgorod is a good example. Even today it has been estimated that an incredible 30–50 per cent of the crops grown annually in European and tropical agriculture is lost to diseases carried by micro-organisms, especially fungi. These disease-bearing organisms, or pathogens, can be spread in a number of ways; carried by larger animals or insects, through infested crops being moved, by living in the soil, or through the agency of airborne spores whose wastage rate is high although this is compensated by the large numbers of spores initially produced. An animal which carries a pathogen without being itself affected by the disease is called a vector and we can find an example of insects acting as vectors in the recent outbreaks of Dutch Elm disease where the pathogenic fungus *Ceratocystis ulmi* is transported from tree to tree by two elm-bark beetles which break down the bark of the elm and introduce the fungus. Partial control of the spread of the disease can be exerted by felling badly-infested specimens and using insecticides against the beetles, but this is not totally effective. Although it seems likely that the present outbreak of the disease (first documented in France in 1918) was attributable to the importation of the pathogen from Asia into Europe, it is quite possible that related diseases were present in antiquity as well. There is a dramatic decline in the elm tree pollen detected from pollen analyses of European archaeological sites and peat bogs around 3000 BC. Various hypotheses have been developed to account for this, including climatic change and the activities of neolithic communities clearing forest and perhaps feeding elm branches to stock. It is certainly true that the elm decline coincides with the appearance of 'weeds of cultivation' (such as plantain) which indicate early agriculture, but the possibility that it was exacerbated by a plant pathogen causing widespread disease in European elms was suggested nearly 25 years ago and has never been disproved. A compound origin for the elm decline seems likely but it would be interesting to analyse a neolithic insect fauna and see if a suitable vector could be identified.

The results of some of these crop failures or diseases may be found in actual human remains; starvation, for example, may result in periods of arrested bone growth which show up in x-rays as opaque transverse lines, called

Harris lines, after their discoverer. Other evidence of chronic food shortage may come in the form of exceptionally slender bones with very light muscle markings often accompanied by much tooth decay and a low age at death. Scurvy, or Vitamin C deficiency, shows up as changes in the palate and gums, and has been identified in an Anglo-Saxon from Norfolk. A case of vitamin enrichment, a diet over-rich in Vitamin A, was found in a two million-year-old hominid skeleton from Kenya which is attributed to a diet too rich in liver and might be support for the contention made above (p. 48) about the need to eat fat as well as lean meat. The effects of Vitamin D deficiency are more familiar to us since one of its manifestations, the disease we call rickets, still occurs today in areas of the world where children have a diet inadequate in milk, fish, oil or animal fats which are the source of this vitamin.- The bow legs characteristic of rickets have been found in the ancient world, even as far back as neolithic remains from Denmark and Norway with a substantial amount of evidence from Roman and later times, including a classic case of a seven-year-old child from the medieval cemetery of St-Helen-on-the-Walls in York.

Disease is an inescapable and integral part of human life, which has influenced early human communities at various scales, from the individual with an attack of mumps to the population afflicted with an outbreak of plague. At the micro scale evidence for certain ancient diseases may be preserved in the skeleton of an individual, but at meso and macro scales such information needs to be combined in order to consider questions like the influence of disease on social attitudes, longevity, population growth and the very evolution of human society itself. Inevitably, the evidence is unevenly preserved. Equal quantities of informative skeletons are not available for each culture, and disease patterns themselves are uneven. More to the point, interest in palaeopathology (the study of ancient diseases from preserved human remains) is quite recent and there are comparatively few experts in this field. Another unfortunate matter is that of preservation; only a small number of diseases actually affects bones, by far the greater number affects the soft tissues of the body which are rarely preserved in the archaeological record except in the case of mummies, either natural or artificial. Indirect evidence of disease may be obtained from coprolite or cess deposits (p. 54), or from the study of historical records. But the systematic study of ancient disease in order to chart its development and comment on its effect on early human communities requires full careful description of preserved bones, accompanied by x-rays where possible, together with examination of bone sections under high magnification and full analysis of hair or soft tissues. The potential rewards are great. We have to remember that throughout history, until very recently, people had little knowledge about the treatment, cause or control of disease. There are a few exceptions to this: the extensive range of homeopathic information doubtless accumulated by most populations, or the ability to perform certain surgical tasks such as the setting of fractures which were always a common part of daily life. Many of the diseases with which we are familiar today never existed in antiquity; rheumatoid arthritis, for example, which is quite common today seems to have been non-existent before Late Saxon times. The opposite is also true; leprosy, smallpox and plague hardly trouble us today whereas they were major influences on world population history.

There is seldom any archaeological evidence for viral disease such as the common cold, which may have been widespread, and almost a complete absence of information for mental disease, or for the subtle effects of disease on an ancient community, such as the need to care (or not, as the case may be) for an afflicted person. This last trait, which was probably a crucial factor in human evolution appears with dramatic suddenness, around 45,000 years ago in burials of *Homo sapiens neanderthalensis*, our cousin. Before that time human communities seem to have possessed neither the resources nor the desire to support group members who were unable to contribute anything positive in the way of obtaining food. Doubtless elderly or infirm individuals were abandoned with what would seem to be callousness, but was in fact essential to survival. Yet neanderthals, for whatever reason, seem to reverse this trend and, in the series of ritual burials associated with neanderthal remains (the first evidence for formal burial), we have the interment of children, adults who have received incapacitating injuries and other non-combatants such as the very elderly. In the Shanidar cave of Northern Iraq (fig. 55) Ralph Solecki found the burial of a male neanderthal who must have been a walking pathological casebook; crippled with arthritis, blind in one eye, with a healed head injury and a right arm, collar bone and shoulder blade which were totally crippled and useless. He must have been fed and supported by his people from the day of his birth, which indicates, for the first time, a sense of communal responsibility and caring, marking, perhaps, the true beginning of humanity.

The skeleton of this individual, coded as Shanidar 1, contains evidence for many different groups of diseases. Congenital birth abnormalities such as his are quite rare, but the group includes such things as dwarfism (*achondroplasia*) which occurs as the result of a gene mutation. The characteristic form of the short-legged dwarf recurs in the art of different periods and is referred to in much historical literature. Skeletal evidence of *achondroplasia* comes from Egypt, both in pre-Dynastic tombs and in the tombs of the pharoahs Zer and Mersekha, as well as several North American examples including the skeletons of male and female dwarfs from the palaeoindian site at Moundsville, Alabama. Such dwarfism is, surprisingly, relatively common (1 in 10,000 live births today and probably the same in antiquity) but other genetic abnormalities may be very rare, such as brittle bone disease (*osteogenesis imperfecta*) which usually results in early death and where only two examples are known, an Egyptian XXIst Dynasty infant and a single Anglo-Saxon. Club foot (*talipes equinovarus*) has been recognised from a British neolithic skeleton and cleft palates from Saxon and palaeoindian skeletons. Hydrocephaly (water on the brain), another congenital disease, is

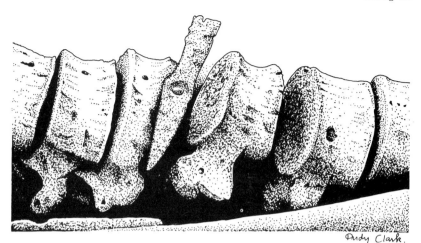

Andy Clark.

32 A fatal wound – the tip of a Roman balista bolt still lodged in the spine of one of the defenders of Maiden Castle, Dorset

recorded in Britain from Romano-British times onwards and there is the skull of a child from prehistoric Nubia with a cranial capacity of nearly 2000cc (the average adult skull has a value of 1300cc). The width of the long bones of the leg suggest that the child was unable to walk, yet it lived into its tenth year – striking evidence of social care for a severely handicapped individual. Arthritis is part of a group of arthritic and degenerative diseases which include everything from spinal fixation by bony growth, first recognised in medieval populations, to the very common osteoarthritis which first appears in prehistory in the spine of a dinosaur, 100 million years old, and is very common both in antiquity and today. At the Mesa Verde site in Arizona, dated to 550–1300 AD, all individuals aged more than 35 had osteoarthritis.

Joint diseases such as arthritis in its various forms are obvious and have often been commented on, even before the modern interest in palae-opathology. Keith Manchester, one of Britain's leading palaeopathologists, notes that as far back as 1897 a description of a Vth Dynasty Egyptian mummy seems to indicate that it had rheumatoid arthritis, although most of the evidence for this disease is quite recent. Gout appears in a male Romano-British skeleton from Cirencester, dated to 150 AD, and this same site has also produced evidence of traumatic disease, the results of injury or accidents. Fig. 32 shows a spectacular example of a trauma, namely a war injury, in this case the bolt from a Roman catapult which was lodged in the spine of one of the British defenders of the Maiden Castle hillfort, found during the excavation of the cemetery by Sir Mortimer Wheeler.

The practice of trephination (removal of an area of skull) is very well documented – over 1,000 archaeological examples are known, some quite horrific. Skull mutilation after death started with neanderthals, as we have already seen. Broken bones were as common a hazard in the ancient world as they are today. Despite the wide range of healed fractures as well as the occasional piece of evidence for surgery, such as the bark splints associated with broken forearms in third millenium Egypt, or some horrendous examples of medieval metal splinting, very little is known of the treatment of fracture. Bones may sometimes yield a cause of death, either obvious (like the balista bolt shown in fig. 32), or more subtle battle injuries such as sword cuts. It is sometimes difficult to tell whether an injury was terminal, although if the sufferer survived for long the growth of new bone can show that it was not.

The archaeological record, always incomplete, may sometimes be positively misleading or at any rate difficult to interpret. Cancer, the most important cause of death today, is hardly evidenced at all in antiquity because its manifestations do not survive well in bone but are found in soft tissues. Even the secondary bone growths caused by certain types of cancer are frequently undetected since they are not obvious unless the bone is x-rayed. The evidence for cancers is therefore rare, except in very obvious cases such as a terrible mouth cancer suffered by an Egyptian of III–Vth Dynasty date, although cancers may have been quite common. Palaeopathologists think, however, that environmental changes such as increased pollution and changing diet are responsible for the high incidence of cancer today, but the origins of this disease could be better documented by detailed examination of skeletal remains using modern methods.

If soft tissues are preserved the range of diseases which may be diagnosed in early burials is greatly increased, but of course this is quite a rare circumstance. Easily the most important group of burials here comes from Egypt, which has produced examples of conditions rare in the archaeological record, such as smallpox, kidney-stones, as well as the rather more common cysts of parasitic organisms such as those which cause amoebic dysentery and bilharzia, together with a wide range of intestinal parasites. Eggs of gut parasites such as whipworm (*Trichuris trichuria*), and roundworm (*Ascaris lumbricoides*) have also been found in pre-Columbian mummies (such as the Peruvian example shown in fig. 33), medieval cesspits and coprolites (fossil faeces) excavated in semi-arid areas, notably in the southern part of the USA.

Despite this ever-growing corpus of information about specific individuals it is, as yet, premature to make any conclusions about the nature and effect of disease in societies from the archaeological evidence alone. Even very well known diseases, such as leprosy (which, although it is caused by a micro-organism, *Mycobacterium leprae*, produces dramatic and highly visible changes in the skeleton) have many unsolved problems. Why, for example, does leprosy, which was a major infectious disease in Roman and medieval times become virtually non-existent, at least in England, by the sixteenth century? Why does leprosy affect only man and the nine-banded armadillo? The skeletal changes associated with leprosy can be very marked, making them easier to identify, as we can see in the medieval Danish examples shown in

33 The pre-Columbian mummies of Peru are usually crouched over in this way. Their soft tissues have provided evidence of a large number of diseases, especially gut parasites like worm infections

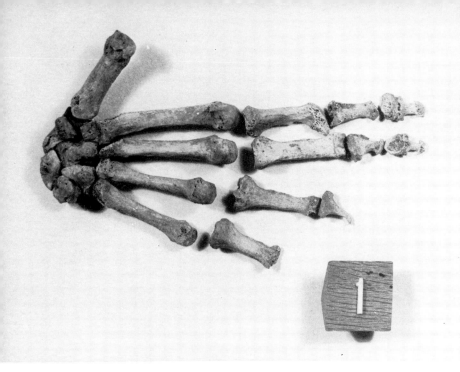

fig. 34, from the Naestved cemetery excavated by Professor Muller-Christensen. The disease affects the hands, feet and face of an individual and can strike him down with varying degrees of severity. The small bones of the hand and feet gradually become reabsorbed, thin and concave in the middle. Eventually, before their disappearance, the bones become pointed at the end, giving the disgusting appellation 'sucked candy syndrome' (fig. 34.1) which does, indeed, describe their appearance very well. A project at present being carried out by Keith Manchester is designed to investigate the frequency of leprosy in an archaeological record, in its different clinical manifestations. Dr Manchester is also interested in the reasons why the disease suddenly disappeared from Europe, although it is still common in tropical countries. He has formed the opinion that the phenomenon is related to the rise in importance of tuberculosis, also evidenced archaeologically, since the two diseases are cross-immune (i.e. someone with leprosy cannot get TB, and vice versa). But leprosy is only one disease, and it will take many years of work with skeletal remains and documentary sources, such as the charters of medieval leper hospitals, to solve just a few of the questions that it produces. Palaeopathology still has a long way to go.

Undoubtedly the most comprehensive small-scale picture of available medical treatment comes from the unexpected find of two small compart-

34 Leprosy mainly affects the bones of the hands and feet. These medieval Danish examples show advanced bone reabsorption resulting in pointed bones ('sucked candy syndrome'), and much damage resulting from ulcers and abrasion

ments on the sixteenth-century wreck of the *Mary Rose* (p. 120) where the ship's master surgeon and his assistant practised their trade. Objects found included wooden ointment jars, ceramic medicine flagons, equipment for bleeding, drug flasks, razors and a urethral syringe contained in a large chest which had sunk deeply into soft muds and silts and was in an excellent state of preservation. This chest, together with a bench, constituted the complete furnishings of the barber-surgeon's cabins. Some of the drugs have been analysed and include an unguent containing frankincense which was probably used for ulcers and fistulas, together with a large quantity of peppercorns which had many medicinal uses from expelling wind to curing 'agues'. Although the blades of the surgical tools had corroded, the handles suggest that surgical knives and saws and an amputation saw had been present. Many of these objects had become mixed up with the surgeon's personal possessions and even his hat was preserved – a simple velvet coif with braid-covered seams and ribbon ties. The position of the cabin on the main gun-deck of the ship is also significant, since the surgeon was clearly expected to be near the action, and the presence of ready-to-use dressings, perhaps plasters, and partially-used jars of ointment (even showing the fingermarks where scoops had been taken out) showed that the surgeon had been busy even during the very short and ill-fated voyage of his ship. This collection of material is the earliest example of medical treatment at sea, the contents described supported by various historical documents including paintings of contemporary barber-surgeons, a medical recipe book of Henry VIII's own salves and ointments and details of the use of urethral syringes (mainly to treat gonorrhoea and bladder-stones) in the works of the sixteenth-century French physician Ambrose Paré. In the *Mary Rose* we have evidence of the treatment rather than the disease, contrary to the usual case, so we must hope that the analysis of the human skeletal material currently being undertaken will give us some idea of the diseases, just to complete the pattern.

Many of the plants which cause disease also have medicinal uses; ergot, for example, can be used to treat bleeding and control migraine. Little is known of the ways in which early communities used plants to treat diseases, although it has been suggested (on the grounds of a pollen analysis from the famous neanderthal 'flower burial' (p. 123) from Shanidar cave in Northern Iraq) that knowledge of medicinal plants may begin as much as 40,000 years ago. At Shanidar all the plants identified by their pollen extracted from the grave sediments are currently used in Iraqi medicine, and one would expect any hunting community to be just as aware of the medicinal uses of their local flora as they were of the plants as sources of food. This is certainly true of contemporary hunting communities, who have an encyclopaedic knowledge of the properties of plants (p. 47).

The use of plants as drugs is also evidenced from the archaeological record, although occurrences are again very sporadic. Hallucinogenic mushrooms were an important ingredient in the religion of many early peoples, two species being predominant, *Amanita muscaria* (the Fly Agaric, fig. 35) and

35 Fly Agaric; beautiful but deadly
and used by the Incas as a hallucinogen

Psilocybe mexicana. The former is poisonous but if eaten in small controlled doses produces visions and hallucinations. In recent times it was used for this purpose by the European Lapps but its importance in prehistoric ritual is difficult to assess without some form of secondary evidence. Mushroom-shaped carvings occur in archaeological deposits in Central America and are thought to be relics of Maya ceremonial, a speculation backed up by pictures in the Maya codices, a series of bark documents which describes religious rituals. But until actual mushroom remains, either in the form of fragments or (more likely) as spores recovered from analysis of the sediments, are found, the use of the Fly Agaric as a drug by the Maya remains an inference. The other hallucinogenic fungus, *Psilocybe*, also seems to have been used as a drug but this time by the Aztecs in their religious ceremonies. Here we are on much safer ground as the practice was noted by the Spanish *conquistadores* in their sixteenth-century manuscripts, which report that the fungus was eaten (accompanied by mugs of chocolate!) in rituals which took place before dawn, and the visions which occurred were then discussed. The cause of the visions, a chemical related to LSD (Lysergic acid diethylamide), was for a long time thought to be non-addictive but has now been shown to cause damage to the chromosomes of regular users, as well as rapid ageing and premature senility.

Not all the drugs of antiquity have quite such drastic effects, and some are attested by good primary archaeological evidence. Hemp was used as a

36 Not a hippie but a fifth-century
Scythian who (appropriately tattooed)
has been going through the hemp-
smoking ritual to purify himself after a
king's funeral. All attested by sound
historical accounts, as well as finds of
the complete apparatus in the Pazyryk
tombs

narcotic by the Scythian tribes of southern Russia in the fifth century BC and
formed an important ingredient of the funeral rites of Scythian kings where,
after the completion of enormous burial mounds such as those at Pazyryk
(p. 136), the tribesmen would feast and inhale the vapour from burning
hemp seeds to purify themselves. Excavation of one of the Pazyryk mounds
produced the complete apparatus necessary for such a rite; poles to support
small felt-covered tents and bronze vessels filled with stones and charred
hemp seeds (fig. 36). In this case we have supporting evidence provided by
the fifth-century Greek historian Herodotus, who obtained a lot of
information about the Scythians in the course of his travels around the Black
Sea. Although his work contains some exaggerations and mistakes, the
picture which he draws of Scythian life has largely been corroborated by
archaeological finds, as in the case of hemp-smoking, although he thought
that the rite was analogous to the Greeks' vapour baths which would have
been impossible without any source of steam:

> In order to cleanse their bodies the men make a booth by fixing in the
> ground three sticks inclined toward one another, and stretching around

them woollen felts; inside the booth a dish is placed on the ground, into which they put a number of red-hot stones, and then add some hemp seed. Hemp is very like flax, only that it is a much coarser and taller plant. The Scythians take some hemp seed, and creeping under the felt, throw it upon the red-hot stones. Immediately it gives out such a vapour as no Greek vapour bath can exceed; the Scyths shout for joy, and this vapour serves them instead of a water bath; for they never by any chance wash their bodies with water.

Since hemp was also used by Scythian shamans (medicine men) to assist them in their religious visions, this curious funeral rite seems more likely to be a cleansing for the mind, rather than the body, and remains one of the few instances where an archaeological record of drug-taking is confirmed by an historical source. Archaeologists have hardly begun to answer questions about the health of ancient communities since we have more evidence for their diet than their diseases, as few of the latter show up in their bones. Disease treatment, except in obvious cases such as the splinting of fractures, will generally remain speculative but the interaction between drugs and disease remains a fascinating one. Nothing is known, for example, about anaesthetics, although we assume that something of the kind would be necessary for patients about to endure the horrors of prehistoric trephination. Did they stun the victims with smoke? Did they use alcohol, hypnosis, orally administered sedatives? Our only hope for answers to such questions lies in the examination of plant residues, but the manufacture of most herbal preparations will probably be archaeologically invisible. We are on safer ground in the historic period where written records of disease treatment occur, although these can often be maddeningly ambiguous. Even when soft tissues are preserved, the record is biased since with a few exceptions mummification was confined to an unrepresentative portion of society. Detailed examination of skeletal records will provide us with further clues, but it seems unlikely that we will ever get an overview of disease patterns and their treatment, only a succession of individual diagnoses.

5
Living

The first human living quarters have left no trace in the archaeological record: indeed, we are not certain what they were like. Mary Leakey claims that an arrangement of stones piled up in Olduvai Gorge over two and a half million years ago is the remains of a windbreak, but it is not until very much later that we have some concrete evidence about early settlement. Much of it is indirect: the residues of former human activities such as hunting or tool-making. The sites may not be 'living' places in the strict sense of the word, but temporary stopping places related to some activity in the hunter-gatherer seasonal round (p. 38), rather than localities which were occupied for any length of time. It is only within the last half million years of human history that we get clear evidence of structures, man-modified living areas, and these are of variable quality and scarce quantity. The oldest is probably Latamne, in Syria, but the best European example comes from a site near Nice, not far from the modern commercial harbour, and was excavated nearly 20 years ago by French archaeologists working under the direction of Henry de Lumley. The excavated area of Terra Amata, as it was named, covered nearly 150m² and produced 21 living floors and over 35,000 artefacts. A programme of environmental analysis, combining the results of soil examination and pollen analysis, suggested that the people who camped at the site around 300,000 years ago enjoyed a temperate climate, a fine sandy beach and an Alpine backdrop with fir and Norway pine coming rather further down the mountains than they do today. The living floors were located in three separate areas and produced the remains of 21 huts, all oval in shape but varying in size from 8–15m long and 4–6m in width. De Lumley considers that he could identify the remains of stake-holes which formed the sides of the huts, supported at the base by cobbles, together with rather more substantial timbers which held up a roof (fig. 37) and living floors composed of organic matter, ash and debris. Each hut contained a hearth and near one of them faecal deposits (coprolite), human in origin, contained plants such as the broom which flower in the late spring or early summer, suggesting that the site was occupied around that time. Mammalian bones, turtles, rabbits, rodents and birds were included in the diet together with some fish. The site, a sheltered cove, might have been selected since it had a freshwater supply and the excavators suggest that the occupation was seasonal, the flimsy huts falling apart after a brief occupation each year for a maximum of 11 years,

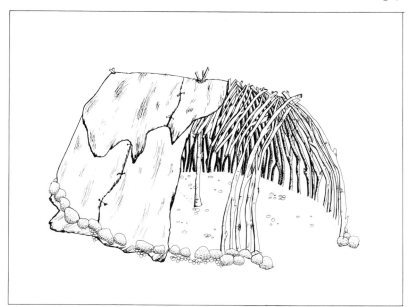

37 The Terra Amata huts were flimsy, made of stakes, with their skin coverings weighed down with large cobbles. They are the earliest dwellings in Europe

and the site being partly obliterated by blown sand (though not entirely, as the huts were rebuilt annually on almost the same spot). It is likely that here at Terra Amata we have the earliest evidence for seasonally organised settlement, as well as a rather complete picture of an 'open' site, preserved and found quite fortuitously.

These 'open' sites, relatively common and surviving well in arid areas such as the Namib (p. 40), are rare in Europe and Asia, where most of what we know about early settlement comes from caves. In caves, as we have already seen, the evidence of animal bones, pollen, sediments and artefacts can be combined to give some picture of the occupation patterns, but little in the way of organic material, with the exception of bone, is preserved. Man did not extensively modify caves, although the occasional stake-hole and rubble pile suggest the construction of windbreaks and internal subdivisions by neanderthal men and later occupants. In many ways we can obtain a clearer picture of early man's adaptability and ability to cope with difficult situations by looking at the way in which he survived out in the open, often in conditions of intense cold. 'Open' site structures are not, of course, representative as they are rare and only preserved in unusual conditions. Some splendid examples do, however, survive, of which easily the most spectacular are the 'mammoth bone' houses of southern Russia, where

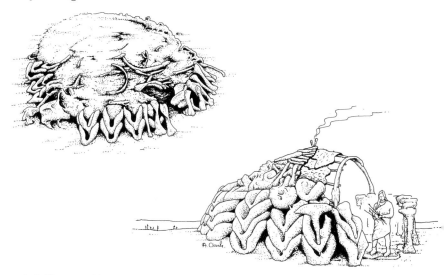

38 Not surprising that mammoths became extinct when you think how many are represented in this late palaeolithic hut from Mezhirich, now reconstructed in the Hermitage, Leningrad

Neanderthal man, and, later in time, representatives of our own subspecies *Homo sapiens sapiens* lived. The remains of these huts have been mainly found in river valleys and the oldest, from the site of Molodova, is dated to more than 40,000 years ago. Early structures seem to have been simple: tents supported by stakes but weighed down with mammoth bones instead of the cobbles at Terra Amata. Later on, entire shelters were made from mammoth bone, including that from Mezhirich, on the River Dnieper south of Kiev, where an oval hut composed of 386 mammoth bones has now been reconstructed in Leningrad. This amazing structure (fig. 38) must be regarded as a splendid adaptation to an environment which was extremely harsh and where wood was scarce. It also gives us some idea of how people lived; the size of the hut (3m diameter) suggesting some form of small family unit, although other evidence supports the contention that whatever the basic unit size, humanity had by that time organised itself into a semi-tribal society, with large groups sharing common tool-making traditions. The existence of these mammoth-bone ruins also suggests a settled or semi-settled type of lifestyle, with higher population densities than those associated with neanderthals or earlier peoples. It is ironic to think that the rising of new social structures associated with fully modern man and the late palaeolithic and evidenced by the development of art styles (ranging from the cave paintings of the Dordogne to engraved objects and small statues from this area in Russia) may have contributed to the extinction of a number of the large herd animals (especially the mammoth) on whom the hunters preyed.

After the last lingering effects of the Ice Age had disappeared in the Near East, by around 9000 BC, the hunter-gatherer people who lived there were faced with a very favourable set of environmental conditions which resulted both in a rise in population density and in the need to organise control over territories in a way that had never been done before. In hunting societies a balance is usually kept between food supply and demand, which itself controls population density, but in really favourable conditions like these the available food supply resulted in such a large population that people were forced to develop new ways of life. One solution was for them to collect in the habitats or ecological niches which best favoured intensive food production but another, better, strategy was to institute a series of gradual social changes resulting in increased social organisation. In these adaptive changes we can see the origin of specialisation, certain members of a community providing services (perhaps connected with the manufacture of goods, or with irrigation, religion or trade) which other people paid for with food. This connection of the development of new social systems in response to increased food production and thus to greater population densities is an interesting one. However, agriculture itself must not be seen as the only reason for the development of settled village (and later town) life, as there are numerous examples of people who developed intensive agriculture but never had permanent settlement. In Mexico, for example, semi-nomadic prehistoric people remained semi-nomadic yet domesticated at least ten different food plants, including maize, by 5000 BC without ever living in a village. Farmers in China, Thailand and Vietnam domesticated plants and animals and invented pottery by the fifth millenium yet their first cities did not appear until 2,000 years later. It all depends on the environment, its resources and the social organisation of a particular people, but the idea that urban life was just the next logical step in the development of 'civilization' – one further link in a chain which started with food-producing villages and the concomitant need to control water resources – is now outdated.

The reasons for the foundation of a village, or later of a city, may be very complex indeed. A settlement may grow up in response to the availability of certain natural resources or at some suitable junction point. At Jericho, a permanent settlement had been established 8,000 years ago, possibly controlling supplies of salt and minerals from the Dead Sea, although the reason for the initial settlement was probably the spring of fresh water which is still visible today. The ancient site is now a high mound (*tell*) of collapsed mudbrick, dust and debris which contains the remains of nearly 10,000 years of continuous occupation. It stands today like an island surrounded by green orchards against the shimmering heat of the Dead Sea Valley and it is not difficult to see what attracted early man to the site. It is still possible to crawl round the edge of the *tell* and see the original spring, still gushing unbelievably clear fresh water at a rate of nearly 4,500 litres per minute, although its destination today is a reservoir for the modern irrigation projects. Although Jericho is nearly 3,000m below sea-level, this water supply made the development of agriculture possible in the area, and by about 9500 BC the Natufian people had taken advantage of the gift, with material equipment for hunting and also for the harvesting and processing of wild grains, a preliminary stage in cereal domestication. Little is known of these early settlers, although they left a shrine behind them on the site, but their successors, called PPNA people (Pre-Pottery Neolithic A), lived on top of the remains of the Natufian settlement in round houses which date from about 8000 BC and which were made of sun-dried mudbrick. It seems quite likely that these round houses were an attempt to reproduce the beehive-shaped huts of the Natufians, since they were replaced in time by rectangular houses more suitable to mudbrick as a raw material. By this time the settlement was a permanent one and the PPNA people felt it necessary to construct a wall for their defence, which, together with a massive irrigation tower, date to the ninth millenium and were probably related to the development of Jericho both as an agricultural and as a trading city which contained around 2,000 people and covered an area of nearly 4 hectares. Its next inhabitants, PPNB (Pre-Pottery Neolithic B), fostered its trading links, not only with the Dead Sea but also with the obsidian sources in Anatolia far to the North, and with the Mediterranean which was the source of the cowrie shells used in the curious plastered portrait-heads found there. Other towns in the area also developed as trading posts, such as Beidha (Jordan, fig. 21) which produced salt and red iron oxide (haematite), widely used as a painting medium both for pottery and people – as paint and also as a cosmetic.

Much of the obsidian handled by these early traders at Jericho came from the curious site of Catal Hüyük in what is now Turkey, where today a 58-foot high mound conceals the remains of a city whose foundation is attributable not to the presence of a good water supply but to its proximity to the sources of this volcanic glass. Had we been able to see the two cities at around 8500 BC they would have presented a marked architectural contrast, since the inhabitants of Catal Hüyük, whose city was excavated by James Mellaart, had invented for themselves a building style which combined strength with the ability to cover uneven ground, but which presented a very curious appearance. The site is a fascinating one, since the excavation was of a standard to permit insights into the lives of the inhabitants, although only one thirty-second of the total area was dug. It seems that the houses were all interconnecting; made of mudbrick and crowded together around court-yards (fig. 39), with flat terraced roofs connected by a maze of ladders. There were no doors – entry to houses or streets came from the roofs, made from a reed mat fitted over the roof timbers and covered with a thick layer of mud

39 Only a small area of Catal Hüyük (A) was excavated, and it may have been the priestly quarter. However, the maze of enclosed courtyards, houses and shrines (B) is unique, and each house was entered via a ladder from the roof (C). After Nellaart (1967)

(A)

(B)

(C)

and then one of white clay plaster, which was repaired each year. The white plastered exterior walls would not be dissimilar to the rooftop view of any Arab town today but the architecture also served a defensive purpose. Catal Hüyük has more rain then Jericho (over 40cm per year) which made it necessary to carry out annual repairs to the mudbrick houses during the course of the long, dry summers with the effect that the houses lasted a long time – Mellaart found as many as 120 coats of plaster on one house from successive annual renovations. Within the house, which was generally a rectangle about 6m by 5.5m, the ladder led down into a living space with plastered walls and platforms of various heights which divided it into working and sleeping areas. The kitchen corner had a low open hearth and an oven with a flat top, with the smoke escaping through the ladder hole. Fragments of cloth had been preserved by carbonisation (accidental exposure to heat in the absence of oxygen which alters organic material to carbon without changing its shape – like the conversion of wood to charcoal), used to wrap the human burials which had been placed under the sleeping platforms of houses or shrines destroyed in a fire dated to 5880 BC. Textiles are very rarely preserved in an archaeological context, especially primitive linen cloths like the Catal Hüyük examples, made from flax whose stems must be soaked to loosen the fibres before being beaten, combed, spun and woven. Carbonised seeds are more common (p. 52), since they may be accidentally preserved in domestic contexts or from grain storage pits.

It seems that Catal Hüyük really flourished from about 6500 BC for about 1,000 years, although its origin lies well back in the eighth millenium. Of the 139 buildings excavated by Mellaart, over 40 seemed to be shrines, some decorated with murals painted onto the white plaster using mineral pigments and with ample evidence for complex ceremonies and religious beliefs. It has been suggested that the function of the town was not a trading one, but that it represented a ceremonial centre, on the grounds that there was an almost total lack of evidence for obsidian working and an extraordinary concentration of religious activities. The excavation of such a small area is, however, unlikely to reveal the full diversity of all the urban activities and different facets of daily life and it is more than possible that Mellaart hit the 'priestly quarter'. We do, however, have some idea of how the inhabitants lived. They had domesticated the dog, and grew wheat and barley. Analysis of seeds, carried out by the Danish founding-father of palaeoethnobotany, Hans Helbaek, identified more than 14 types of domesticated food plants of which two different species of wheat (einkorn and emmer) predominated, together with barley, bread-wheats and peas. Helbaek noticed a difference in the appearance of the two major cereal crops, the einkorn grains being small and irregular and in fact quite similar to the wild einkorn which grew in the area, suggesting that the species had only recently been domesticated. The emmer wheat grains, on the other hand, were larger and more uniform, suggesting that they had been domesticated rather earlier. Shepherd's purse and another mustard-like herb were also grown for their oily seeds which were important to early farmers, although today their place in our diet is taken by other plant oils such as linseed, groundnut or olive oil. Fruits included the hackberry (which was made into wine by the Romans) and nuts such as acorn and pistachio which could not have grown on the level plain surrounding the site but must have been gathered from trees on the foothills of the mountains several miles away. The dry conditions which preserved these seeds also preserved the remains of their wooden containers, often made from either oak, juniper or fir cut from the surrounding forests using polished stone axes and shaped very simply by hollowing out solid wooden blocks. Although well preserved in waterlogged conditions (where air and the bacteria which cause decay are excluded) wood does not survive well in great heat, and requires immediate conservation if it is not to disintegrate after excavation. Reed baskets and matting also served as containers and seem to predate the use of pottery (once thought of as an essential component of settled village life in the Near East). Meat obtained from domesticated animals such as sheep, goat and cattle was supplemented by hunting of wild cattle (aurochs), deer, boar and wild ass and other wild species including fox, wolf and leopard which were probably hunted for their pelts.

It seems that the prosperity of the settlement in Catal Hüyük was attributable to its profitable trading in obsidian. Like all early cities although simple in social, economic or political terms, it clearly relied for its survival on both its local catchment area and much more distant links to other urban centres. In a more developed form, but reflecting the same trends, early urban communities gradually concentrated wealth and power into the hands of a few individuals. This was then recycled in the form of the major building projects, both private and public, which characterise later cities as well as the maze of laws, literature and bureaucracy which marks the passage of the city into history. Adjustments to the urban system can be the result of changes at many different scales, for example the digging of new pits or wells, the construction of new buildings, altered drainage or land-use, or improved communications. People, like rabbits, have a constant need to dig holes for numerous reasons; deposition of rubbish, obtaining water, sanitation, building foundation, tanning pits and graves etc., but this makes such sites extremely difficult to excavate. Towns are the most complicated sites in the archaeological record, being complex, multi-functional, more-or-less-permanent settlements which may have been continuously occupied for thousands of years. Towns will include great social stratification from extreme wealth to extreme poverty, provide a marketplace and manufacturing place for a wide variety of artefacts and crafts, and a diverse variety of habitats connected with the different functions of the town which may include administration, defence, recreation, and trade. No two towns are alike, even twentieth-century planned towns, and no two have the same degree of archaeological visibility. Each has its own set of archaeological problems and priorities and each will yield different types of information varying with the characteristics, position and complexity of the site.

Excavation at a small British seaport may produce a quantity of information concerned with the diet, economy and lifestyle of its medieval inhabitants but excavations in part of the City of London may give a window onto the administrative centre of 2,000 years of government. It is all a question of scale.

The intensity with which towns are occupied, and the tendency to reuse both land and buildings, may produce very thick (and much disturbed) deposits. At York, with an average population estimated at 10,000 during 57 generations since the founding of the city in AD 71, the debris of 570,000 lifetimes is concealed within less than 120 hectares, not all of which (perhaps fortunately) is available for excavation. The waterlogged nature of many of the York deposits, combined with excavation programmes specially geared to recovering information about ecofacts, has resulted in an incredibly detailed view of the changing face of the city and its inhabitants from Roman times until the present, on a scale as yet unequalled in England. However, this embarrassment of riches has not yet been completely analysed, nor is it likely to be. After eight years of continuous excavation at York the volume of animal bone alone which has been recovered would, if only 20 seconds were devoted to each bone, take someone 27 years to evaluate. But the information obtained will be of immense importance, not only in indicating the food requirements of its inhabitants, but in all sorts of minor matters such as the availabilty of animal by-products (bone, antler, horn, fats, glue, leather), the choice and selection of the animals used, the ratio of wild/domestic animals, what pets were kept etc.; the list is endless.

A look at fig. 40 illustrates some of the problems faced in interpreting urban deposits – the material will have come from a wide variety of habitats outside, as well as inside, the town. Both natural agencies (like the wind) and human activity (people harvesting crops and bringing the grain into the town) will transfer material from outside the town to contexts within it, and it may often be very difficult to disentangle the origin of the deposits. The evidence provided by insect faunas has been very helpful here, since the wells and cesspits so commonly found in European towns, at least of medieval date, provide nice waterlogged conditions for their preservation. The separation of insect remains via a paraffin flotation will produce a mess of tiny fragments which may take some time to understand, but since the different insect species are highly indicative of specific habitats and microenvironments, they can give us a picture of the microenvironment of the town; whether or not there were piles of standing rubbish, what kind of industries were practised and what the interior of a building was like. Like all branches of environmental archaeology, insect identification is highly specialised (at the time of writing there are only five such specialists in England) but much interesting work has been done on urban deposits, especially at York.

An alternative example of an urban excavation with different sets of problems and in a very different environment would be the work done in the medieval Russian city of Novgorod, located some 150km south of Leningrad.

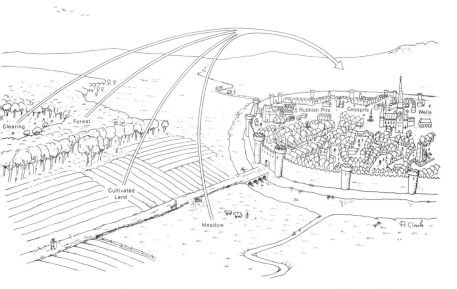

40 The rubbish deposits in towns may receive material from many sources, representing different environments around the town as well as inside its walls. Pollen, for example, may be blown in and grain, rushes and other plants will be brought by human agency

It was occupied from the tenth to fifteenth centuries and, like many Slav towns, had its origin around a castle/hillfort containing the royal palace and cathedral (*kremlin*, in Russian). The medieval town grew up around the *kremlin* on land bounded by the river Volkhov on one side and a small stream on the other, and the nature of the deposits is such that they preserved vast quantities of information from different contexts, enabling the habitats of the town to be reconstructed on a variety of scales. A further bonus was that much was known of the medieval history of Novgorod from its own Chronicle which covers the period 1016–1471, although the uppermost archaeological layers are later than this and major changes in the town plan were carried out between 1723 and 1778. Novgorod (fig. 41) was an important political, economic and cultural centre made almost completely from wood, whose excellent preservation has permitted the reconstruction of houses, workshops, stores, quays, palaces and streets at all periods, with their associated artefacts. This is a very rare archaeological occurrence and enabled Russian archaeologists to produce a picture of life in Novgorod which could not have been obtained from the documentary record alone, complete with little human details like the children's toys and the shape of medieval chessmen. Twenty-eight separate street levels and their associated structures were preserved, each street having apparently been relaid simultaneously throughout its entire length. These roads were of the corduroy type (logs laid

41 The wooden world of Novgorod, at level 8 (dated 1369–1382). The main corduroy roads were bordered by log-cabin type houses with several rooms, often joined together to make complex multi-storey buildings transversely side-by-side), a form of construction which goes back to at least the fourth millennium in Europe and which was used for trackways crossing boggy ground in the Netherlands and western England when the first farming communities had hardly arrived. At Novgorod such roads provided a platform for sledge-runners both in winter and summer, and it seems that wheels were very little used. The periodic relaying of the streets was necessary not as a response to fire, as might be thought, but to solve the problem of rubbish (when the accumulation of dung and domestic waste in the houseyards became critical another level was merely added to the streets).

The town lies near the edge of the north Russian pine forest zone and most of the houses were of pine, although other woods were apparently used for fences, furniture and 101 types of household utensils. Oak or larch was used for the stove substrates and house construction was very simple (in a region where straight conifers abound), using an axe to notch the end of the pine logs, and packing the corners with chips, bark and moss to give a tight fit. Log ends were always chopped, never sawn, since chopping squeezes the wood-fibres and delays decay while sawing has the opposite effect, opening up the tissues. House construction was very rapid, and lobbies (fig. 41) were used to link frame to frame and make huge buildings. At certain religious feasts it is recorded that an entire church had been constructed in a day, and in 1262 the Chronicle says that the entire town was rebuilt afresh, which is not impossible. A great contrast exists between the simple carpentry required for this method of construction and the complex timber-framing used in medieval English buildings of the same period, where a frame, usually of oak, supported vertical panels of laths and plaster, requiring elaborate mortice-and-tenon joints and a complex roof.

At Novgorod the Russian peasant house had several parts (fig. 41); a heated cabin (*izba*), a lobby (*seni*) and an outhouse (*klet*) and was normally two- or three-storied. The plot on which the house was built was very different from that of an English medieval town; more like a rural farmyard than a square, neatly aligned to the street, in the English model. Excavation showed that the yards were apparently never cleaned and new buildings were raised only by a layer of twigs over the heaps of dung. Moreover, there was a positive incentive not to let the layers of sludge in your yard fall below that of your neighbours – you received all his rainwater! The yards were so untidy that whole objects (sledge-runners, doors, complete logs) had become lost and as the ground surface rose outside the lowest part of the timber box-frame, it sometimes became buried in the deposits. Although this produced excellent preservation of artefacts, it must have made living conditions rather unhealthy, although the stove located at the back of the cabin opposite the door would have generated considerable amounts of heat. A unique series of more than 400 birch-bark documents has survived, chiefly messages, lists and memos which were thrown away and survived merely by chance, but which give a tantalising glimpse of Novgorod life. Fig. 42 shows two examples: Document 134, 'Order from Gregory and Domna and Repekh. Get the log

42 Birch-bark documents Numbers
134 and 337 from Novgorod survive
because of the damp burial conditions.
They can be anything from a note to
the bailiff to a declaration of intent

cabin and outhouse ready and send Nedan into Luga and Ilin today';
Document 377, 'from Nikita to Ulyanitsa. Marry me. I want you and you
me. And as witness will be Ignato ...'

Houses were ventilated simply by fitting perforated blocks into the wall
logs, which is fortunate since despite the frequent documentary references to
baths no bathrooms were found. The use of buildings could be inferred from
work residues and great continuity of tradition was evidenced, in contrast to
Winchester. Shoe-makers and leather-workers lived for the majority of the
eleventh to fourteenth centuries in the same area of the town, and during
the whole of the eleventh century blacksmiths worked in yards near the
intersection of High and St Cosmos and Damion Streets (the church
dedicated to these two patron saints of blacksmiths was located in that
sector). Despite this complex organisation no central system of drainage or
water supply was ever instituted (cf. York, fig. 43). A picture of the life of the
inhabitants could be built up from the finds which included agricultural and
fishing equipment like sickles and trident-ended fish spears. The good
preservation of leather produced a whole range of footwear types from
slippers to boots, together with complete sets of equipment for tanneries and
leather-working. This sort of evidence is quite often found on urban sites, as
the medieval examples from Austin Friars, Leicester show us (figs. 44–5). Vast
seed samples from Novgorod were analysed to find out the agricultural basis
of the town (in the thirteenth- and fourteenth-century layers alone nearly 24
million seeds were found by dirt-processing), showing that the Novgorod
hinterland grew mixed cereals with barley and rye, wheat being rare and
wheat flour doubtless constituting a luxury. This large seed sample, with over
one million grains actually examined, showed that agricultural practices had

43 Stoutly-built Roman sewer at York, whose rich deposits have produced a wealth of information about the life and times of legionnaires in the fort

changed over the 500 years; correlations could be made between changes in weed seeds from freshly-reclaimed land and weeds of established arable land. Long-term use of the same fields was indicated and the season of crop sowing could be determined. An overall picture of a thriving farming community was obtained, meadows around the town being used for hay, and crops being grown more than 5km from the settlement as the nearer ground was not suitable for agriculture.

The citizens of Novgorod lived in a wooden world; had wood not survived it is impossible to estimate what our picture of life would have been, but it would be grossly distorted. The bonus of documentary records and tree-ring dates linked to the Chronicle makes its chronology secure. We even have a good idea of the relationships between the town and its hinterland which were, as always, symbiotic; to provide, for example, a market for the agricultural produce of the surrounding area which, in turn, feeds the inhabitants of the town. However, as all the needs of the citizen cannot be met from his nearest town, this necessitates trade and travel between urban

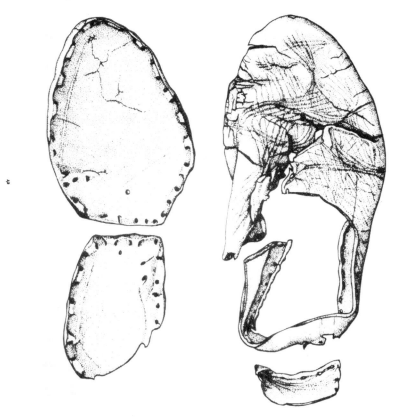

44 Medieval leather shoe from Austin Friars, Leicester

centres, sources of particular raw materials and central administrative areas. Novgorod traded with the Mediterranean, as we have already seen (p. 72), and with the Middle East. Like all towns it was the nexus of a complex web of trading networks, at local, regional and international level.

Towns are essentially an historic phenomenon, although many would argue that the hillforts of the European Late Bronze Age and Iron Age constituted at least proto-urban sites. Purists would also argue that the central places of advanced civilizations such as that of the Incas do not constitute towns in the strict sense of the word, because they did not possess written records and are, therefore, to be defined as prehistoric. But these are semantic quibbles.

Evidence of the internal organisation of towns does sometimes survive relatively undisturbed. The best example must, of course, be Pompeii, where life came literally to a dead stop on August 24, 79 AD, as a result of the eruption of Vesuvius which buried the town under a mess of ash, pumice and volcanic

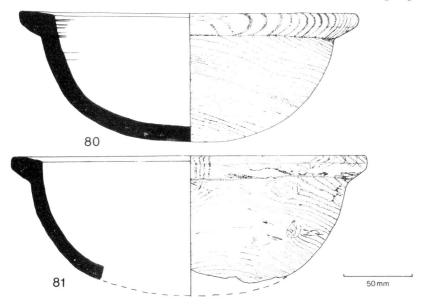

80

81

50 mm

45 Wooden bowls from the same site. Note the archaeological convention of drawing them with 1/4 cut away

mud. This resulted in the preservation of the town's activities at one specific moment in time; tables set for breakfast, posters for the next municipal elections and a cross-section of all the arts and crafts. Although the splendid preservation of so many Roman towns, especially those in North Africa, has resulted in many detailed pictures of Roman town planning and precise details of domestic architecture, at Pompeii these really come alive. Fig. 46 shows the market garden in the House of the Ship *Europa*, with its plants in pots, vegetable gardens and network of paths and water cisterns. This was just one of the large stretches of market garden which combined the growing of vegetables with straight rows of fruit trees and areas for bedding out young plants. Other excavations showed gardens associated with villas that were lavishly planted with trees and shrubs, which on analysis could be identified as olives, lemons, soft fruits, pomegranates, walnuts and bilberries, with chestnuts and vines grown on trellises. The organic evidence, in the form of pollen analysis, could be combined with preserved wall-paintings which show charming scenes of outdoor dining-rooms, shaded by large trees, overlooking courtyards with fountains. Excavation has revealed the drainage system and complex of baths.

Baths were exceptionally important in the Roman lifestyle and we are fortunate in possessing many fine examples from different sites, including some in Britain. These vary from the small domestic variety to the great bathing complex investigated by Barry Cunliffe at Bath itself. Roman public

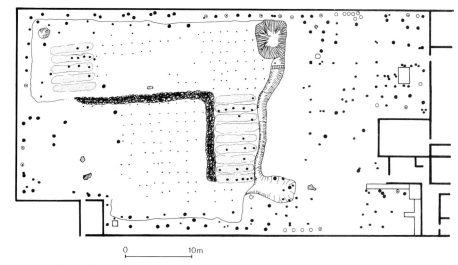

46 Plan of a market garden at the 'House of the ship *Europa*' in Pompeii. Small dots are vineroots, black dots roots of other kinds. In the centre of the garden (dark shading) is a neat path with parallel vegetable beds to its right, and in the top right corner a small circle marks the site of a water cistern

bath-houses, which had facilities for relaxation as well as hygiene, performed an important social function in the Roman world which John Wacher, one of the leading authorities on Roman Britain, described as 'akin to a good club'. In Roman Britain public baths seem in many cases to have been top priority in the construction of new towns and such bath-houses were often on a very large scale. At Leicester, for example, there was a huge bath complex including an exercise area (*palaestra*), latrines, plunge bath and rooms on the 'sauna' principle at different temperatures (fig. 47). The Leicester baths, like many other Roman-British examples, were fed by an aqueduct and their design incorporated thick walls and roofs to insulate against heat loss and keep the different rooms at their correct temperatures. At Bath, where nearly a quarter of a million gallons of water per day bubbled up from a spring into a reservoir to supply the bath complex, adequate drainage systems were clearly required, involving the construction of a main drain connected directly to the water source through which the overflow could be removed, and which also received waste water from the various baths at intervals. The system was planned on a large scale, using stone slabs sometimes measuring as much as 60cm by 90cm, so that the main drains were large enough to permit men to walk along and clean them out periodically.

Such sewage systems are not unique to Bath; there is a magnificent example from York, perhaps the best in England, built of huge stone blocks (fig. 43). Analysis of the insect fauna from the York sewer deposits showed

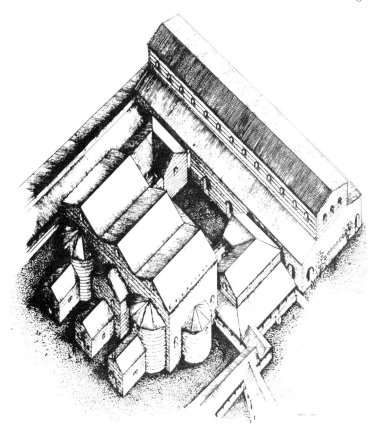

47 The Roman bath-house, Leicester, temperatures
with its range of rooms at different

that it not only drained the latrines and bath house but was also located near a grain warehouse, indicated by several insect species which are pests of stored grain products. The baths, which are not still in existence, were also supplied with water through an aqueduct and the whole system drained out to the River Ouse. This is undoubtedly the most complete example of a Roman sewer in England although others are known, including a fine specimen from Lincoln and a timber-lined sewer from Cirencester. Bath provided an example of Roman plumbing at its best, with a complex of lead water-pipes and ducts, but eventually the drainage system broke down as a result of a rise in sea-level (and thus in the water-table) during the late Roman period. The great bath complex and associated temple of *Sulis Minerva* gradually silted up. However, little environmental work has been attempted since the excavations were carried out piecemeal and generally

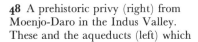

48 A prehistoric privy (right) from Moenjo-Daro in the Indus Valley. These and the aqueducts (left) which supplied the water were stoutly built of brick

some time ago. Nevertheless pollen analysis of a black organic mud sealing the floor of the temple precinct contained plant species characteristic of wet places such as *Typha* (reedmace), *Cyperacaea* (sedge), and a silt lying on the basement floor of the hypocaust at the east end of the Baths was identified as the result of the system becoming flooded by spring water as the drainage system became unable to cope. The sewage system at Bath has a curious parallel in what is undoubtedly the earliest system of municipal drainage ever constructed, not in the Roman world but 3,000 years earlier in the cities of the Indus valley civilization in what is now Pakistan (fig. 21). At Moenjo-Daro, for example, the town was planned on a rectangular grid system with its streets each accompanied by neat brick-lined open sewers, complete with basins (periodically cleared out) to catch debris which might clog the sewer, and connected to each house via an open gutter. Fig. 48 shows one of the covered aqueducts which supplied the houses with water, together with a neat brick sit-down privy of surprisingly modern appearance. These privies were connected to the drains, which also carried off bathwater from the many private bathrooms via clay-lined pipes which led into the sewers; an extraordinary system for the time.

Moenjo-Daro provides one of the few exceptions to the generalisation that the inhabitants of early towns were little concerned with drainage and sanitation. We have already seen the example of Çatal Hüyük (p. 94) where the enclosed courtyards served as repositories for all the domestic waste from the settlement. One reason for this is that early settlements, even the first towns, were seldom planned, and without any formal planning they tended to grow up as a heterogeneous collection of buildings whose inhabitants were responsible for the disposal of their own rubbish. Human communities make a very great deal of rubbish – in the 1980s an average of 50,000 tonnes of rubbish are discarded daily from English households, 90 per cent of which is dumped as unsorted landfill in rural areas. Very little recycling is done despite the fact that the average rubbish bin contains, during the course of a year, enough waste paper to save six trees and enough food waste to keep a garden in compost as well as half a tonne or more of glass, metal and plastic whose recovery would cut energy and waste disposal bills. This lack of systematic planning for waste disposal, horrifying though it may be in a hi-tech society, is far from new. There are only a few examples of systematic planning where someone has given thought to such matters as regularising water supplies and drainage.

Sewers, garderobes, cesspits, latrines and rubbish pits are fascinating to the environmental archaeologists; how better to tell what an early community was like than by studying its discarded rubbish? Drains, after all, not only remove cess but carry away all the residues of domestic, commercial and industrial life. It is not surprising that bioarchaeologists have developed such an affection for sewage deposits (the subject of many tasteless jokes from their colleagues), when such contexts can produce so much interesting information. Take the post-medieval sewer at Amsterdam, recently described in a review article by the botanist James Greig, which produced an amazing list of fruit including grapes, raspberries, blackberries, strawberries, pears, apples, figs, bilberries and gooseberries from its deposits. Clearly, some of these are exotic fruits which were imported but, apart from rare contemporary recipes or historical accounts, we have little information about the minutiae of ancient diets unless we look at such remains. Apart from food plants, a large range of herbs and spices (poppy, mustard, mallow, linseed, coriander, caraway, dill and fennel) have been noted from sewage which we presume were either eaten or used for medicinal purposes. Sewage may also give some idea of what diseases ancient physicians had to cure; the eggs of roundworm and whipworm are often very common, and tapeworms and liverflukes also occur. Not all cess is human waste; some is the debris of food preparation, but these types of rubbish are often mixed up together, and all sorts of other things added as well, such as the debris from sweeping rushes off a floor, or cleaning out a stables. Archaeology has often been defined as the science of rubbish, and in the case of cesspits this is certainly true.

Towns, like living organisms, are continually growing and modifying themselves wherever possible. This can (hopefully) be detected from the stratification but life is made a lot easier if there are documentary records. Martin Biddle, working at Winchester (Hants, England) had sufficient documentary evidence available to establish the use and ownership of nearly all the properties within the town, and various dates in the eleventh and twelfth centuries, which showed a horrific range of occupations within quite small areas as well as significant and drastic changes of function over the period. This sort of detailed reconstruction would be impossible from the archaeological evidence alone, but an archaeologist assisted by the historian makes a potent combination. No other British town has quite so much supporting documentation as Winchester, but excavations at a number of others (London, Durham, York, Norwich, Northampton, Lincoln, Gloucester, Carlisle etc.) are beginning to make quite a body of evidence. Comparison of information gained from excavation in these centres (which is not, alas, based on equal quantities of excavated data or equal funding) will gradually lead towards the possibility of studying and comparing whole urban systems at different scales and at different points in time. At the moment, in western Europe, we have acquired (as a result of the almost compulsory excavation required in the teeth of urban redevelopment programmes over the last 20 years) a few very well studied sites and a number of other 'windows' on urban landscapes. Future archaeological work, with less resources, seems likely to be concentrated on particular problems, perhaps on specific structures, areas or periods, defined as the result of model-building and testing so that the dichotomy between town sites whose habitats are completely recorded and well studied, and towns where they are known only from the evidence of artefact, structure or document, will disappear.

6
Moving

The first form of land transport was human power, in the form of backpacks or the use of dragged sledges, of the kind shown in pictograms used by the Sumerians before 3000 BC. Such simple means sufficed quite nicely when the heaviest materials to be carried were the material equipment of a hunting community, but with the development of farming and its rapidly expanding demands, new, improved transport facilities were required. Different societies have different transport needs. The archaeologist Stuart Piggott pointed out some years ago that wheeled vehicles would only be invented by societies who needed to move heavy or bulky loads across flat landscapes. Other prerequisites are a suitable supply of timber and the right animal to pull the vehicle. Not all successful societies utilised wheeled transport; the Inca Empire, which until the creation of the Pan-American highway held the record for the longest road in the world (their trunk road down the Andes), controlled their vast empire and mountain road network without wheeled transport (which was, in any case, unsuited to the nature of the terrain) using networks of runners who could transmit messages 380km in 24 hours. Llamas were their only pack animals and are not strong; they can carry a load of only around 45kg at a time, travelling 16–30km a day. But they can live off the sparse vegetation in the High Andes and have additional uses as suppliers of wool. Their general inefficiency as pack animals is the reason for the suggestion that their initial domestication, sometime during the third millennium BC in Peru, was for ritual reasons, since they played an important rôle in Inca religion as sacrificial animals. The lack of suitable domesticates, and the difficult country, meant that the complex Inca civilization needed to use manpower in its vast building projects, moving the huge neatly fitting blocks so characteristic of Inca architecture from quarry to destination by hand. Of course people are an efficient means of transport; the pyramids, for example, and the great megalithic monuments of Europe including Stonehenge, were built using huge co-ordinated gangs of workmen and relatively simple tackle of ropes, rollers and sledges. The Inca empire is full of surprises – half the agricultural staples of the world today were first domesticated by the Incas. Some of their building projects survived until quite recently; the famous bridge of San Luis Rey in the Andes, made of twisted rope 45m long across a deep gorge between two precipitous mountains was still in use in 1890, 540 years after its construction and having seen the collapse of the empire of its makers, partly as a result of the introduction of a new animal, the horse.

The establishment of the horse as a means of transport during the second millennium in Europe and perhaps 1,000 years earlier in southern Russia and western Asia revolutionised the way people lived and communicated. It also had considerable implications for the development of warfare and the speed by which communications between population centres could be achieved. The dramatic social changes which follow the introduction of the horse are evidenced from recent times in America, where the lives of the Plains Indians were transformed within a few generations by their acquisition of horses from defeated Spanish invaders in the late seventeenth century. Surprisingly, very little is known of the wild horse from the end of the Ice Age until its domestication in the fourth millennium BC (initially as a food animal) and today these wild horses are represented only by the *Equus feres prezewalski*, Prezewalski's horse, which is said to survive in the Mongolian steppes, although recent suggestions indicate that it may now be extinct in the wild. Small-sized descendants of this wild horse are used by the Mongol nomads today, both for transport and as sources of food (p. 67). The ancestors of these incredibly tough horses transported the Mongol armies in their conquest of half Europe and Asia in the thirteenth century. Domestic horses occur in Late Neolithic sites in Europe but become much more common after 2000 BC and throughout the Bronze Age. By far the largest numbers of horse remains have come from Russian sites where, by at least 1500 BC, there seems to have been a differentiation between northern pony-type horses and Arabian types. Even so, most domestic horses in the ancient world were rather small, less than 14 hands. The smaller 'Celtic' ponies which are found in Britain, western Europe and Greece were much shorter than this, often less than 1m high at the withers.

The earliest known ridden horses date from the fourth millennium but the evidence is secondary – tomb figurines, paintings and carvings. It does, however, seem likely that the development of riding took place around 3500 BC in the steppes of southern Russia or the Caucasus, but no first-hand archaeological evidence of this comes until the ninth century BC with the rise of nomadic societies such as the Scythians, Sarmatians, Huns and Mongols. The tombs of Scythian kings in the Altai mountains contain the remains of tall well-bred geldings complete with saddles, bridles and head-dresses and appeared to have been bred for taller bodies and longer, slimmer legs. We must see the rise of the ridden horse as a means by which a human community extended its control over territory, to establish a highly mobile, self-contained lifestyle based on flocks and herds. Only later, but as a result of this development, did the ridden horse provide both the cause and the means for the rise to power of the mounted warrior. The horse was used as a draught animal before it was ridden, and breeds of horse continued to be used for this purpose after the development of riding. One of the Scythian graves contains a wooden burial-carriage which required four horses to draw it, but long before this date small pony-type horses were harnessed to chariots to provide transport for the élite in the earliest civilizations of Mesopotamia and Egypt. Chariot horses became common in the Middle East during the second millenium BC, and it used to be thought that they superceded an animal called the onager which is frequently depicted in Mesopotamian art. Onagers, wild ass-like equids, were probably not domesticated but interbred with donkeys and (later) with horses, and used for drawing chariots, carts and sleds. It is often thought that the domesticated onager was the forerunner of the chariot pony but some doubt has now been cast on this, and many of the larger, heavier carts and sleds of the Middle East at this time (for example the funeral sled of Queen Puabi [Shub-Ad] from Ur) were actually drawn by oxen. Although two- or even four-onager chariots appear in art they may never have occurred in real life. The heavy slow oxen were used as draught animals, nearly 5,000 years ago and domesticated, probably for that purpose, around the same time as the emergence of those early agricultural communities already discussed (p. 59).

The first wheeled vehicles were heavy carts equipped with solid, disc wheels either cut from a single massive piece of wood or made from three pieces joined by dowels and mortices. Lighter vehicles with spoked wheels are more recent, and associated with the horse. The erratic preservation of wood has meant that we do not have a complete archaeological record of those first wheels, although a number of isolated examples are known. In Russia a second-millennium solid-wheeled cart and wagon was found at a site near Lake Sevan. Not all wheels are found in burials, although these are by far the most common. Several one-piece solid disc wheels have been found in Denmark and the Netherlands in boggy contexts, dating to before 2000 BC, and identical to examples from cart burials in the Russian steppes. One example, 645mm in diameter, was found associated with the remains of a trackway dating to 3840–55 BP at Nieuwe Dordrecht in Holland. This trackway, representing one of the very earliest examples of 'roads' was the 'corduroy' type, made of poles laid at right-angles to the direction of travel. There is an equally early British example called Abbott's Way, in the low-lying area of the Somerset Levels, just north of Glastonbury. Here a major project designed to record and study the ancient trackways crossing the area has been under way for many years, directed by John Coles of the University of Cambridge. The Somerset Levels project is a 'rescue' operation, initiated because peat cutting in the area had revealed tantalising fragments of buried trackways, used since the arrival of the first farmers to cross the marshy ground. The project, actively assisted by co-operative peat-cutting firms, has been working not only on the trackways but on the peat deposits in which they are stratified, building up a picture of climatic and environmental change from the preserved pollen, insects and plant remains.

Abbott's Way is the earliest track of the 'corduroy' type and would be suitable for wheeled transport. Other construction methods include baulks of timber laid transversely but covered with brushwood and twigs to help

49 The Meare Heath track, Somerset Levels, whose erratically spaced timbers were firmly pegged into the surface of the bog, and would have been covered by brushwood to prevent wheeled transport slipping

against slipping. Some trackways were merely footpaths, planks laid across the bog and carefully pegged into its surface, just to facilitate people crossing from one piece of dry ground to another. Others were made of woven hurdle-work laid on the bog surface and provided evidence of prehistoric woodland management, the coppicing and pollarding of different trees, especially hazel, to get twigs and stakes of the right size. Fig. 49 shows a section of the Meare Heath track, made of oak, birch and alder planks rather irregularly spaced, and fixed into the bog with pegs, finally covered with brushwood to prevent slipping. Twelve hundred metres of this track have now been seen, but some of the others are even longer. All the tracks were made for the same reason, to help human communities cope with very damp terrain, either by making footways or by the construction of simple droveways for cattle or surfaces suitable for wheels. It is another example of cultural adaptation to a tricky set of environmental conditions. One might ask, but why did anyone want to live in such a wet area at all? The answer lies in its ample supplies of fish and wildfowl, forestry resources and grazing on the 'islands' of dry ground which made the construction of the trackways worthwhile. Similarly, the need to control and feed a vast empire caused the Incas to build their road network and terrace their mountain sides to grow (among many other things) more than 200 varieties of potato.

Each culture adopts the means of transport best suited to its needs (conditioned, of course, by any technological limitations). Mongols living in the steppes or the Gobi fringes, draw their worldly goods along on camel carts (fig. 50); people living near lakes, rivers or the sea naturally invented boats to travel and transport their goods. The very earliest stages of water transport are often evidenced in the archaeological record only from tantalising glimpses, like the wooden paddle found at the Mesolithic site of Star Carr (Yorkshire), presumably for propelling an eighth-millennium canoe, or the Egyptian reed boats shown in phaeronic paintings and reconstructed by Thor Heyerdal. However, there are now more than 20 examples of British

50 Bactrian camels transporting a
family home, Mongolia

dug-out canoes, all from waterlogged deposits and most dating from the third
to fourteenth centuries, together with many plank-built boats. Some
examples of the latter are caulked with moss, such as the Bronze Age boats
from North Ferriby, Yorkshire, where the moss species *Polytrichum commune*
(Hedw.) was stuffed between the planks to aid in making the boat watertight,
and also used in the manufacture of rope.

Other common types of caulking include a mixture of animal hair and
wood tar, found in the Skuldelev ships (below). Bronze Age waterfronts are
also known, including a famous example from Runnymede, on the upper
course of the River Thames, where the bank had been reinforced with
vertical oak posts and a brushwood ramp during the ninth to eighth centuries
BC. This early interference with the local ecological balance seems to have
affected the nature of fluvial silt deposition, and the establishment of what
was interpreted by the excavators as a small trading settlement suggests that
trade on the Thames may have started very early indeed.

The many excavated medieval examples of plank-built boats include the
Blackfriars specimen (fig. 51), but plank-built boats dominate marine and
coastal transport in north-western Europe from quite an early date and there
is a series of splendid post-Roman examples, including the Viking ships
salvaged by Danish archaeologists from the bottom of Roskilde Fjord at
Skuldelev in Denmark, 30km west of Copenhagen. The collection included
two warships of which one (ship 2) was a Viking longship and the other (ship
5) a rather smaller warship; two trading vessels, one large (ship 1, figs. 52 and
53) and one smaller (ship 3) together with one fishing boat (ship 6). Of these
the small warship (5) could be paralleled with a ship excavated from the

51 The Blackfriars ship

barrow of a Viking chieftain at Ladby on the island of Funen in 1935, only in that case the timbers were very poorly preserved and the mere outline of the ship remained, complete with rusty nails. A full-size replica of this Ladby ship was made in 1963 and has cruised successfully in each succeeding summer, permitting a number of experiments to be carried out concerned with its seaworthiness and steering qualities, and even with loading and unloading of difficult cargoes such as horses. Ships very similar to Skuldelev 5 are shown on the Bayeux tapestry and carried the men and horses responsible for the Norman Conquest. Skuldelev 2 and 4, which were found to be part of the same longship, are the remains of a large ocean-going warship nearly 30m long and 3.5–4m wide; the sort that carried Viking raiders to the coast of England. Other famous examples are found in the spectacular Viking boat burials at Oseberg, Tune and Gokstad. Wet timber is not always easy to conserve; if the wood is allowed to dry it will shrink and crack. Skuldelev 1, made of pine and lime woods, was the easiest to conserve and the other ships, made mostly of oak, were the most difficult. But the whole project required the careful washing and measuring of each piece of timber, followed by prolonged soaking in polythelene glycol (wax) baths which gradually replaced the water in the timbers, preventing shrinkage and deformation.

Earlier boat excavations in Denmark, carried out without the benefit of this plastic-impregnation technique had resulted in the near destruction of the finds. The Hjortspring boat excavated from a peat-bog on the island of Als in 1921–2 was made of limewood and the timbers were so soft that one could easily poke a finger through them. Wood conservation techniques of the time involved boiling the timbers in a saturated solution of alum but it has since been found that after a while the timbers begin to crumble again. However, the Hjortspring boat has been re-treated by the removal of the original alum and replacement by a more effective preservative. The conserved timbers of the Skuldelev ships have been reconstructed where possible, and the five ships now stand in an air-conditioned environment at about 20°c and 65 per cent humidity, in the Viking Ship Museum at Roskilde. Although the five Skuldelev ships differ widely in construction and proportions they have certain features in common; all are clinker-built (of riveted overlapping planks) and all have the same type of reinforcements and frames. Studying them, and comparing them with other finds, gives a picture of European shipbuilding from 300–1300 AD.

Close examination of the timbers of ships may give clues as to how they were used; for example the marked wear and tear on the lower planking of Skuldelev ship 3 suggests that she was run up on sand or shingle beaches. By contrast, the tenth-century Graveney boat excavated from Kent has a very smooth keel-plank, probably due to its being berthed on the mud of the Thames estuary. The Graveney boat is of special interest to the environmental archaeologist because of its cargo. It was a merchant ship, with a capacity of about seven tonnes and seems to have been involved in North Sea trade. The most plentiful plant remains obtained from its interior suggest that it carried a cargo of hops (*Humulus lupulus* L.) which were probably used for brewing; indeed, by the time that the Domesday Book was written the monks belonging to the Abbey of St Augustine in Canterbury had obtained a reputation for liking their beer, and it seems possible from the Graveney material that British hops were being traded, perhaps across the Channel, from a very early date.

Over recent years much attention has been focussed on the archaeology of waterfronts which can provide evidence of a town's origins, growth, decline and trading patterns. Because of the likelihood of waterfront deposits having good conditions for ecofacts, significant advances in environmental reconstructions have been made. A waterfront is an economic indicator and includes all sorts of different habitats such as wharves, quays, jetties and docks as well as the remains of streets, houses and (sometimes) churches and palaces. Waterfront archaeology may also turn up the remains of ancient wrecks and ships' timbers, which help in studies of nautical architecture, and waterfront sediments may give clues about the silting-up of ports and harbours. Research in London has illustrated the nature of the port from Roman times onwards where excavations through the sometimes 10m deep deposits, which cover a total area of some 8ha, have produced windows on the

commercial activities of London until the present day. Similarly deep waterfront deposits have been excavated in Europe, 6m stratification at Hamburg and a very early post-Roman waterfront at Gdansk, Poland, being merely two examples.

Whole ships are sometimes found, such as the splendid broad-beamed sailing vessel with a shallow draught which was wrecked in the Thames during the late fifteenth century and recently excavated near Blackfriars, London (fig. 51). It seemed to have sunk near the contemporary river wall, of which another section was visible at the Trig Lane site, and its flat-bottomed single-masted shape suggests that it was just used for local trading. By a fortunate circumstance it has proved possible to examine how it was loaded

52 Excavated fragments and the
reconstructed skeleton of Skuldelev 1

and unloaded, since excavations at the nearby site of Barnard's Castle
produced the complete rectangular plan of a fourteenth- and fifteenth-
century London dock, near the medieval castle and surrounded by stone
walls, lined by stout oak posts to protect moored boats from snagging against
the rough stonework (fig. 54). Several phases of rebuilding were indicated
and a reconstruction of the complex made from the excavated remains
suggests that it included a dock, unloading area and warehouse. Analysis of
the timbers used for waterfront structures in Britain and north-west Europe
shows that oak (*Quercus* sp.) was the preferred species, because of its strength,
durability and water-resistance. Elm (*Ulmus* sp.) and ash (*Fraxinus* sp.) are
also found but are comparatively rare. As many specialists have commented,

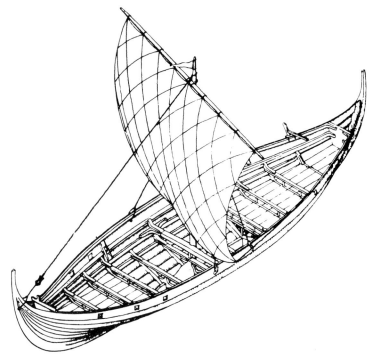

53 Skuldelev 1 might have looked rather like this, a small coastal trading boat, stoutly built

oak is easily the most common tree in medieval archaeology and comparatively easy to recognise in a hand specimen, preferably confirmed by cutting a section through the timber to examine its structure; if excavators could learn to identify it, much valuable laboratory time and expensive packing material could be saved. The study of oak timbers from well-preserved waterfront structures in Britain is currently being carried out at the University of Sheffield, where specialists are not only investigating the use of tree-ring dating techniques (dendrochronology) to make a chronological framework for the timbers, but also trying to build up an archive of information about woodland history and wood technology.

Of course the most famous event in nautical archaeology of recent years has been the raising, in 1982, of the Tudor warship *Mary Rose*, from the sea-bed outside the town of Portsmouth which she had left 400 years ago after a very short voyage which terminated ingloriously on July 19, 1545. The bulk of the post-excavation processing and conservation of the *Mary Rose* material lies in the future, but we already have a detailed picture of life on board. The *Mary Rose*, a 700-tonne warship with 91 guns and the second largest ship in the navy of Henry VIII, was stationed at Portsmouth as part of an English

54 The Blackfriars ship and its wharf in London. Note the strong revetments on the wall and range of buildings (all having different uses) behind

fleet designed to repulse a French attack in July, 1545. On July 19, before sailing, the ship suddenly keeled over and sank rapidly with a loss of over 700 men. Eyewitness accounts of the event are available, a most unusual circumstance in any type of archaeology, as was the exact time and position of the wreck. Sixteenth-century salvage attempts, for the ship and its valuable contents, failed and the ship gradually collapsed into the sea-bed. Chance exposure of the timbers led to the rediscovery of the site of the wreck in 1836 and systematic underwater prospecting resulted in the planning, excavation and finally the raising of the remains of the *Mary Rose* which is at present in dry dock at Southsea, awaiting reconstruction and full exhibition to the public.

The *Mary Rose* project undoubtedly ranks as one of the most important underwater archaeological projects ever undertaken and its director, Margaret Rule, carried it through with thoroughness and persistence and, in the final stages, under the full glare of media interest and television cameras. The reason for the immense amount of public concern can only be speculated on, but it is estimated that nearly ten million people watched the live televised broadcast of the raising of the ship, not only for the technical brilliance of the feat, which involved the underwater construction of a vast steel cradle, on which the wreck was positioned before raising, but also because the *Mary Rose* project had that spark of glamour so often missing from modern archaeological work, although present in the major spectacular sites excavated towards the beginning of this century. The interest was also there because the *Mary Rose* was a time-capsule, preserving the recognisable remains of peoples' way of life (and death) for 400 years. Such 'windows' on early life are, after all, the goal of modern archaeologists, but it is often difficult to tell, merely from looking at an excavation in progress, how the buried pieces of information can be assembled. Here, a graphic picture of the sailors' lives could be seen from the good preservation of the galley, complete with a stack of pine logs for fuel and a large tub with wooden plates and bowls. Behind the mainmast, seamen's and officers' chests were found complete with all their personal possessions, beside boxes of arrows and a barrel of candles. Guns, navigational instruments, spare rigging etc. were all passed along for conservation.

It will be many years before all the finds are processed – in archery equipment alone 2,000 arrows, 138 bows and 12 wrist guards have been found since 1979 and Ann Stirland, a human skeletal biologist, is currently working on the bones of their owners. The remains of more than a hundred people have been found on the ship and an examination of their bones in conjunction with their clothing and associated weapons will produce evidence about standards of diet, nutrition and hygiene, projects which must be completed before a full understanding of the site is obtained. The astonishing find of the intact barber-surgeon's cabin (p. 86) illustrates the excellent state of preservation of much of the information. All kinds of small personal touches illuminated the life of the seamen: hand-lines and fishing floats in the seamen's chests to pass away the time, the remains of a backgammon board complete with counters, many musical instruments and items of clothing. But the importance of the *Mary Rose* as an example of 'transport' lies not just in the well-preserved fabric of the ship itself but in the unique circumstances in which it sank and was raised. The result is a living museum of Tudor life at sea, so much more than mere timbers, and, thanks to good preservation and excavation, probably the most important underwater archaeological project ever undertaken.

7
Dying

Deliberate burial of the dead is a uniquely human characteristic, which appears quite abruptly in the archaeological record around 70,000 years ago, associated with neanderthal man. We presume that pre-neanderthals disposed of their dead rather casually, perhaps leaving them for scavengers, and even neanderthals are unlikely, judging from the small amount of burials found, to have interred all the members of a group. The fact that they buried any at all is most interesting, since deliberate interment, often accompanied by the burial of objects such as stone tools or joints of meat, suggests a sense of ceremony or ritual and perhaps some kind of belief in an afterlife or spirit world, for which it was necessary to provide the dead with food and tools for their journey. This idea culminates in the incredibly complex funerary rituals practised in many civilizations, notably those of Egypt. Surprisingly, the first burials are not necessarily those of males who might have been group leaders, but often those of children or the elderly. At Teshik-Tash cave in Uzbekistan the body of a neanderthal child had been surrounded by the horns of mountain goats held upright by stones, and the whole structure covered with earth. At Shanidar cave (fig. 55) in Iraq there are a number of neanderthal burials, one of whom, Shanidar IV, had been buried in a grave accompanied by bunches of brightly-coloured wild flowers. Lewis Binford, (p. 31, above) has challenged the interpretations placed on some of these burials on the grounds that the primitive nature of some of the excavations does not allow for such factors as the importance of identifying disturbance, of animal origin, in cave burials. However, there can be little doubt that many neanderthals were, indeed, buried with considerable care and concomitant ritual.

Over the succeeding millenia burial rites have changed, often according to custom or fashion. In the present day, for example, cremation is a more popular method of disposing of the dead than inhumation, while 100 years ago the reverse would have been true. During the neolithic period in southern England multiple burials in a communal tomb called a long barrow sometimes occurred. Over 200 such barrows were constructed between 3500 and 2000 BC, containing an estimated 1,500–3,000 burials with an average of half a dozen individuals per barrow. The barrows probably functioned as ossuaries, since they seem to include the disarticulated remains of people who died at different times, and presumably their relatives practised some rite like

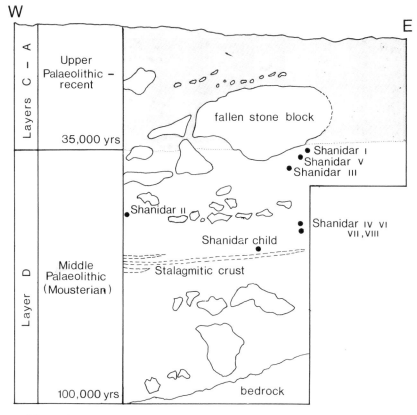

55 Many of the neanderthals who were buried in Shanidar cave had died there, some as a result of roof falls. Shanidar I is the old, crippled individual and Shanidar IV the controversial 'flower burial'

exposure of the bodies before collecting the bones into a communal tomb. The long barrow itself was merely the end of a complex ritual carried out over a long period. This is a further manifestation of the paradox which exists in neolithic society between extremely simple material culture based on farming and small agricultural settlements, and highly complex social structures capable of communal activity such as the construction of vast henge monuments and the ability to sustain long-term trading links.

At Fussell's Lodge long barrow in the west of Salisbury Plain the remains of over 50 individuals were found, inside a timber mortuary enclosure which was located at the end of the 30m long barrow (fig. 56). Paul Ashbee, the

56 Fussell's Lodge is a splendid example of collective burial in a long barrow. The bones were collected into groups within the mortuary house, whose large entrance posts can be seen on both plan and reconstruction

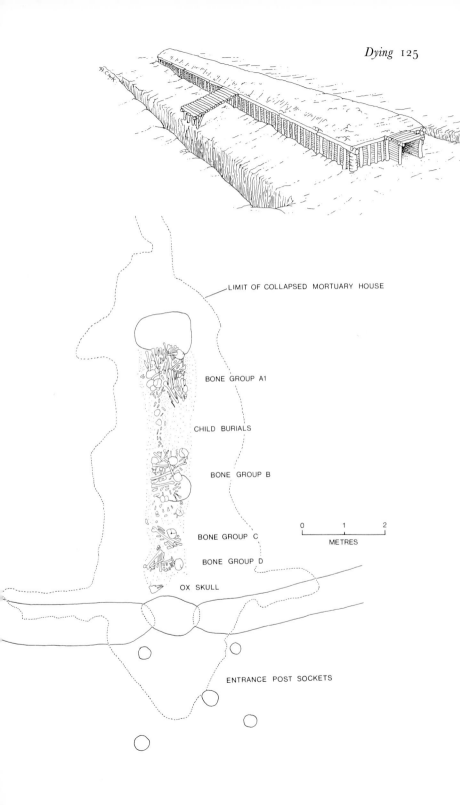

LIMIT OF COLLAPSED MORTUARY HOUSE

BONE GROUP A1

CHILD BURIALS

BONE GROUP B

BONE GROUP C

BONE GROUP D

OX SKULL

0   1   2

METRES

ENTRANCE POST SOCKETS

author of a standard work on long barrows, calculated that over 21,000 cubic metres of chalk had been dug from the ditches, which, when one considers that the palisade timbers totalled at least 660m, (excluding the 45m of massive timbers in the mortuary house), together with more than 600m of smaller timbers behind (fig. 56), indicates the massive nature of the work. Some of the tree trunks, which reached 4m in length, would have weighed over two tonnes and produced a transport problem comparable to the blue-stones in Stonehenge. Competent planning and working by organised labour gangs, at everything from timber-felling to ditch-trimming is indicated, together with considerable skills in surveying; the Fussell's Lodge mortuary house, for example, is exactly aligned with the axis of the enclosure and the entrance causeway. At Fussell's Lodge long bones and skulls had been stacked seperately into specific groups (fig. 56) within the four bone-stacks, presumably representing different episodes of packing into the mortuary house. Such disarticulated bones might have been exhumed from previous burials, which would account for the admixture of broken pottery fragments, bone and soil which could not be explained away as the result of the collapse of the mortuary house. This was not, however, the case in all earthen long barrows. At Wor Barrow (fig. 3) and Nutbane, for example, articulated skeletons were found, which suggests that intact corpses were buried; very different from the assemblages of bits and pieces of defleshed bodies such as those from Fussell's Lodge. One skeleton, from the Maiden Castle barrow, seemed to have been decapitated either before or after death, accompanied by mutilation of the legs and arms, although this is an isolated example. Other barrows contain cremated remains, or mixtures of inhumations and cremations, although there does not seem to be one traditional burial rite but many different ones. It is sometimes difficult to work out the number of individuals buried in any one barrow, and the figure for Fussell's Lodge could be between 53 and 57. These included 14–15 adult males, 15–16 adult females and 22–24 children, with the adults being all probably under 50 years of age at death. This degree of uncertainty is far from rare in reports on burials. The nature of the burial, whether single or multiple, the quality of the excavation, and the state of preservation of the remains, influence the kinds of questions which can be answered by the archaeologist examining it.

Communal burial is not confined to prehistoric contexts. Fig. 57 shows two views of the interior of the bone crypt in the parish church of the village of Rothwell, Northamptonshire, which houses bones disinterred from the graveyard when the church was extended in the thirteenth century AD, as well as other bones from the nearby Jesus hospice which was built in the sixteenth century. The situation is in many ways analogous to that of a long

57 Literally stacks of long bones from the crypt at Rothwell Parish Church, Northamptonshire. Their analysis will tell us much about the medieval population, if it is carried out before the bones are destroyed by fungi and flooding

barrow – communal reburial of the remains of a large number of people at a considerable time after their death, but at Rothwell, as at other ossuaries, the sample size is very much greater and it is estimated that the Rothwell crypt contains the remains of perhaps 20,000 people. Rothwell poses a fascinating problem for physical anthropologists but it is one that must be tackled quickly, since the huge stacks of long bones (each over 7.5m^3 in volume) assembled when the crypt was reorganised in 1900 AD, are gradually disintegrating in the damp conditions and as a result of the immense pressure put upon the bones at the base of the stacks by the sheer weight of material above. The only remedy is complete drying-out of the crypt and the full conservation of each bone, followed by storage in controlled conditions, but such procedures are very expensive and it is possible that much of the valuable information from the Rothwell bones will be lost. A pilot study was undertaken by Charlotte Roberts, with the object of obtaining some information about the population of Rothwell at different periods: the diet, diseases and general characteristics of the local inhabitants. A major aim was to see if the two groups of reinterments (thirteenth- and sixteenth-century) could be distinguished from detailed bone measurement and the processing of the statistical results using a computer. Results were encouraging. Many of the bones showed interesting pathological features (p. 80) including evidence for arthritis, fractures, Paget's disease, tuberculosis and different infections. The sample size was, however, too small for generalisations about population characteristics and it is to be hoped that more work on Rothwell can be undertaken before the immense collection dissolves as a result of periodic flooding of the crypt and attack by fungi.

Such an immense and well-dated bone sample could then be compared with other medieval populations, such as the cemetery of St Helen-on-the-Walls in York, the twelfth- to sixteenth-century cemetery of Clementhorpe (also in York) and many other sites, to see if any significant regional or chronological differences emerge. Church and churchyard archaeology has recently become a major branch of the subject, since the presence of an historic monument such as a church enables all sorts of useful correlations to be made between the detailed documentary records generally kept of the local population and its representatives buried in the churchyard. The scale of detailed information obtainable from such studies is several orders of magnitude greater than that produced by the careful measurement and description of a single burial. We are moving from micro to macro scale and attempting to reconstruct some aspects of the life of an entire population (or at least the fragment of it which was buried in a churchyard) rather than describing in detail the physical characteristics of isolated individuals, however intrinsically interesting. It is unfortunate, therefore, that in contrast to the long barrows and ossuaries described above, the majority of prehistoric burials (when, in the absence of historical records, we are even more dependent on the evidence provided by the skeleton) tend, like the Iron Age example from Danebury shown in fig. 58, to be single inhumations rather

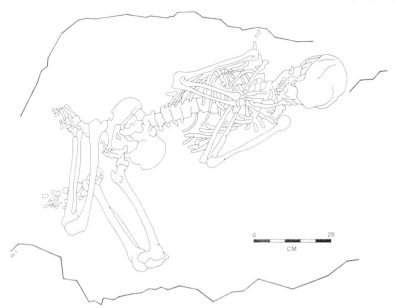

58 An Iron Age burial in a reused storage pit from Danebury, Hampshire. The hands appeared to have been bound across the chest, since there was some crushing of the wrist bones and a brownish sediment which might have represented a binding thong

than family vaults, although there is a very early Neanderthal 'family cemetery' at the cave site of La Ferrassie in the Dordogne.

There are, of course, many exceptions to this gross generalisation – ranging from small simple inhumation groups at almost all periods, sometimes under mounds called barrows, to rich ceremonial burials accompanied by complex grave goods, such as the sixth-century Iron Age example from Hohmichele in Germany where a nobleman and his wife had been buried on a timber platform under a large mound, together with many of their ornaments and personal possessions, including a wagon and a nest of bronze cauldrons. The excavated material and a reconstruction drawing are shown in fig. 59. At the opposite extreme, but rather earlier in date, are the large cemeteries of the Deverel-Rimbury culture of southern Britain where, around the ninth century BC, the preferred rite was to inter the cremated remains in a large pottery urn, sometimes inserted as a secondary burial into an earlier barrow, and sometimes assembled into large flat cemeteries. The practice of cremation does not mean that all is lost for the anthropologist studying the remains – prehistoric cremations were notoriously inefficient, being carried out on open fires instead of the modern closed ovens, and the results often include quite large fragments of bone, sometimes enough to identify the age

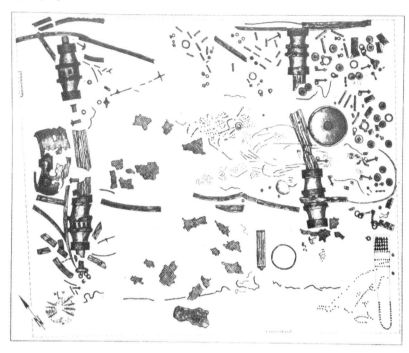

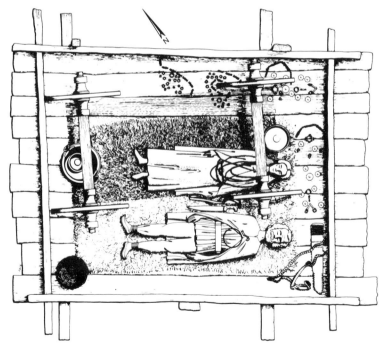

and sex of the individual, together with other features including his blood group and palaeopathological features. However, dealing with cremations is a slow and complex business and few people are qualified to undertake it.

Fashions in burial rites, such as the modern change from inhumation to cremation, can change in a very short time and for no reason that is apparent to the observer, separated from the society in question by hundreds, if not thousands, of years. For example, in the Early Bronze Age, burials associated with the 'Beaker' people (so called from the characteristic drinking cup which they placed in their graves) which occur in the early part of the second millennium BC tend to be single graves often covered by a round barrow; very different from the communal burial in long barrows practised by their predecessors. A difference in burial rites may indicate a major social change rather than a new fashion, and in this case close examination of the skeletons suggests that the 'Beaker' people were physically quite distinct in appearance from the native neolithic farmers and may represent an intrusive group.

The more numerous the burials of a culture the larger the scale of information that may be obtained from them. For isolated individuals we are limited to such matters as evidence of diet or disease, calculation of height, establishment of blood-group, sex and perhaps the cause of death. With larger groups we can get an impression of mortality rates among different elements of the population by careful measurement and comparison of bone data. This sounds a lot easier than it is; any physical anthropologist will comment on the difficulty of establishing even the simplest facts for an early population, partly because the data is unrepresentative and partly because it is necessary to make comparisons with modern populations which may have been affected by different variables. As we have seen, the survival of soft tissue is very rare but so is the survival of the bones of newly-born children (neonates), which are very fragile and often not buried in the same place as the rest of a group. The bones of a newly-born Bushman infant, dated to around 500 BC, were recently excavated from a hut circle site at Sylvia Hill, on the ocean fringe of the Namib desert in South-West Africa. The skull (fig. 60) was almost paper-thin and the whole body so small that it could be comfortably packed in the cardboard cylinder which had been wrapped round a wine bottle, for transport back to the laboratory.

The neonate was one of three burials excavated in 1981, in the course of a field survey project designed to map the hut circle complexes of the area, and examine the midden deposits (p. 49) associated with them. It was found that the hut circles were occasionally reused for burial, the bodies being crammed into depressions in the hut floors and weighed down with stones for some protection against predators such as hyaenas (fig. 61). No grave goods were

59 Cart burial from Hohmichele. Remains of a couple (largely represented by their ornaments) on a solid wood flooring and accompanied by very rich grave-goods. But why is she lying under their cart?

60 Tiny skeleton of a newly-born Bushman infant from Sylvia Hill, Namibia, with bones so fragile that they were almost impossible to excavate

found, but all three burials (including the neonate) had been made in the contracted (foetal) position, presumably to save space. Radio-carbon dates for the skeletons shown in fig. 61 are 510 ± 45 BP (Pta–3294) for G1 and 1070 ± 60 BP for G2, but the neonate, which was associated with G1, could not be dated because to do so would have required the whole of the fragmentary skeleton. Dates from other hut circles within the complex, which seem to have been used seasonally by Bushmen/Hottentot (Khoisan) communities to exploit seafood, range over 800 years indicating that the settlement was sporadically occupied for a long period. Both the adult skeletons here were identified as male, a fact which surprised the excavator (me) in view of the association of G1 with a newly-born infant, and the difference in height and weight of the individuals. The rather fragmentary skeletons had been much affected by the damp conditions of their burial, which is clear from the sketches.

In such a case the physical anthropologist reporting on the bones was able to comment on racial affinities as well as age, sex, weight, disease etc., but this is not always possible. It is sometimes difficult to establish the age of an individual at the time of his death but it does seem that the mortality rate for ancient peoples was much higher than for modern societies – probably due to advances in diet and medicine. The anthropologist will often be able to establish the cause of death if it is a wound or disease which leaves some mark on bone, and age at death can be found from an examination of tooth eruption, closure of the sutures of the skull and fusion of the epiphyses (ends)

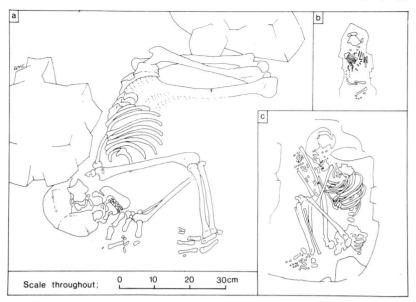

61 Three Bushman burials from Sylvia Hill, all compressed into hollows in hut floors and covered with stones

of the long bones with their shafts, which occur at known ages in modern populations. Tooth wear and the onset of age-related diseases such as some kinds of arthritis may help the process even more with adult skeletons. Violent death is rather easier; at the Romano-British site of Larkhills, Winchester several individuals had cut marks on their neck vertebrae and their heads placed near their feet or between their legs. This could mean two things; either that decapitation was the cause of death, or that the heads had been removed after death as a sacrifice. The two interpretations would be archaeologically indistinguishable, but in this case the pathologist decided in favour of the latter on the grounds that the neatness of the cut (exactly between the third and fourth vertebrae) suggests post-mortem removal.

Ritual murder or sacrifice is also evidenced from the archaeological record; the early excavations of Sir Leonard Wooley at the Royal Cemetery in Ur, Mesopotamia, showed that the rulers had been buried with many hundreds of their subjects; a feat which could hardly have been accomplished unless they went voluntarily. The archaeological record shows no sign of violent death and all the bodies are neatly arranged in lines with their head-dresses in place (fig. 62), perhaps the victims of an executioner or the administration of some drug. Preservation of soft tissues would have been of the greatest help here, but is rare except in conditions of extreme dryness (where the tissues become desiccated), damp waterlogged burials (where the

bacteria which cause decay are excluded), or, very rarely, when they have become frozen.

The Royal Scythian graves at Pazyryk, in the Altai mountains, which have already been mentioned (p. 88) provided a splendid example of this last circumstance: a natural deep-freeze. Many of the tens of thousands of burial mounds raised by the nomadic horsemen have been plundered, either in antiquity or fairly recently, but some have now been properly excavated. The Pazyryk tombs, first investigated by the Soviet archaeologist Sergei Rudenko in 1929, then again from 1947–1949, form part of a fourth-century royal cemetery. In the example shown in fig. 63 the actual log-built burial chamber lies at the foot of a 3m-deep pit, covered by a low mound composed of the dirt removed, capped by piles of boulders. Although the area in which these tombs were found, near the border of the Soviet Union and Mongolia, is south of the zone of permanently frozen subsoil, it becomes very cold in winter and the cold air sank down into the tomb, froze and occupied the space between the boulders. Since the brief summer is insufficient to melt the now solid mass of ice, the area around the burial chamber became perpetually frozen, preserving its contents almost completely intact. The very fact that the tombs had been looted contributed to the preservation as the grave-robbers' shafts let more cold air into the burial chambers which eventually froze, preserving an almost complete record of the way of life of the nomadic Scythian tribesmen. Nearly all the fragile organic materials (fur, wood, leather and textiles) survive intact, together with some of the bodies of the dead. The freezing process seems actually to have been quite gradual; in the grave shown in fig. 63 food offerings buried with the dead had decayed, but the skin and hair of the corpse was in remarkably good condition. The acceleration of the freeze after the entrance of the robbers who had disturbed the chief's coffin and scattered his bones about, had occurred relatively soon after the original burial in the fifth century BC. Some of the valuable objects were undoubtedly looted, but a cave-in seems to have cut short the robbing of this particular burial, although others were almost completely destroyed.

It is difficult to overestimate the importance of such finds. Even in this case, with the descriptions of Herodotus available (p. 88), we would not have known the facial features of individual people, nor their hair colour. One of the Pazyryk chiefs had long, black wavy hair and one woman had red hair; one chunky chieftain had been extensively tattooed and his body covered with animal patterns which were, in many cases, replicated on the jewellery and ornaments which accompanied him. All had been embalmed by removing certain internal organs and careful stuffing with grass, moss and herbs, the corpses being placed, sometimes in pairs, in decorated coffins made of larch wood. The deep-freeze preserved their clothes (generally laid on top of the

62 Before and after. Carts, oxen and their attendants wait for death in one of the Royal Tombs at Ur. Original reconstructions by A. Forestier, published in *The London Illustrated News* of June 23 1928

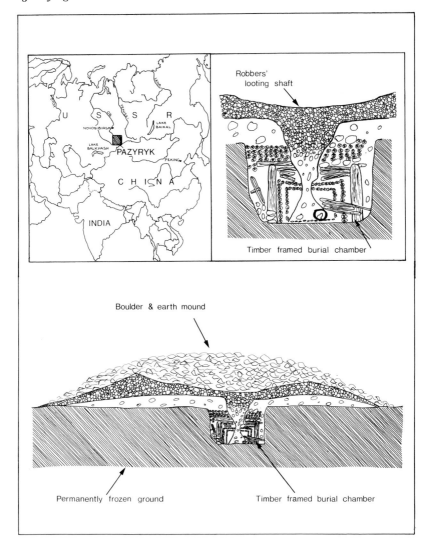

Robbers'
looting shaft

Timber framed burial chamber

Boulder & earth mound

Permanently frozen ground   Timber framed burial chamber

63 The Pazyryk shaft graves, which have produced a unique picture of fifth-century Scythian life, are one of the rare examples of a natural deep-freeze. The fragile organic materials, and the bodies, survived entombed in ice at the bottom of the timber burial chambers, covered by a stone mound which had condensed the cold air and frozen the tombs

bodies) including shirts made of a type of linen, tunics of patchwork leather and felt leggings with heavy soles. One woman had boots of leopard skin with bead embroidery on the soles, and some had peaked felt hats. Much of the household paraphernalia was preserved, including rugs, mats, saddle-trapping and wall-hangings often dyed bright colours, embroidered or covered with appliqué decoration using plant and animal designs. Most of this material is now in the Hermitage Museum, Leningrad, where it encapsulates the lifestyle of these nomadic people and stresses the similarities between their lifestyle and that of their descendants, the Kazakh and Mongol horsemen of today. Political changes have, of course, initiated social change but the basic way of life remains much as it was, even if the running stag pattern embroidered on Scythian rugs from Pazyryk survives as the emblem of a popular variety of motor cycle, and decorates many a Mongolian front mudguard!

Preservation in a natural deep-freeze is, of course, very rare, but a rather spectacular example has recently been described from Greenland, where two medieval Eskimo graves, containing the bodies of six women and two children, were discovered in a remarkable state of preservation by two hunters in a crevice on the north shore of the Nugsuak peninsula overlooking the Umanak fjord on the west coast of Greenland. A full examination of the remarkable find (to be published in book form next year) has now been carried out by more than 50 Danish and Greenland scientists. A date of 1475 ± 50 has been obtained for the group, whose tissue-types indicated that they might be related, and analysis of the faecal remains in one woman suggested that she had died in July or August: the only time when the mountain sorrel (whose pollen was identified in her gut) would have been in flower. The causes of death were varied; one of the older women appeared to have had a naso-pharyngeal cancer, a toddler had a pelvic disorder which was destroying his thigh-bone. Apart from these specific diseases, no definite causes of death could be established, although drowning or succumbing to some kind of epidemic remain favoured hypotheses. The excellent preservation of the bodies revealed all sorts of facts about life in medieval Greenland; infra-red photography of the mummies showed, for example, that the women (except the youngest) had their faces tattooed in different patterns, accomplished by drawing a soot-covered thread through the skin. Stomach contents suggested that these people utilised wild fruits as a component of their diet: cranberries, blueberries, mountain sorrel and knotweed.

But it was the clothing that came as perhaps the greatest surprise, including extraordinary undergarments composed of feathers from different bird species (fig. 64). Feathers are rare in the archaeological record, although examples are known from arid environments, often from coprolite, which makes this find all the more important. An inner hood of delicate feathers from the red-throated diver protected the head, with arm pieces made from porous young cormorant skins reinforced in the forearms by mallard feathers. 'Thermal vests' covered these, based on young cormorant

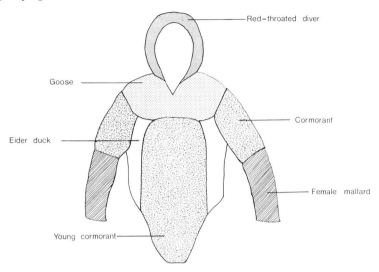

Red-throated diver

Goose

Cormorant

Eider duck

Female mallard

Young cormorant

64 The medieval eskimo women recently found in Greenland were well equipped to face the cold in these feather garments which they wore inside their coats. The feathers and skins came from different species, each chosen for some particular property such as extra warmth (eider duck) or flexibility (cormorant). After Pearson (1984)

skin with the bird's neck hanging downwards. Side pieces came from the eiderduck and extra protection was afforded to the neck and shoulders by goose feathers. In addition to her feather vest the well-dressed medieval Eskimo woman wore neat sealskin shorts, and one had a cloak made of 48 separate sections of reindeer skin, carefully chosen and assembled with due regard for pattern, colour and style. Short 'parkas' made from the skin of the ring seal had cuffs trimmed with fur. Footwear consisted of reindeer-skin stockings with the fur next to the skin, sometimes containing a dune-grass inner cushion, covered with sealskin outerboots which had been water-proofed with seal oil and urine, all carefully sewn together with seal sinews rendered pliable by chewing. This extraordinary find illuminates the daily lifestyle of this small family group. They lived by hunting whale, reindeer, fish, sea birds and seals more than 500 years ago, illustrating that even in the harsh Arctic conditions of medieval Greenland fashion was not forgotten and that man is not only able to adapt to such harsh conditions but to flourishing there, developing a complex material culture.

Human soft tissues and other fragile organic materials are sometimes preserved in 'freak' conditions, such as the leather cap and miner's knapsack 'pickled' in an Iron Age salt mine at Hallstatt, Austria, or the well-preserved medieval corpse (fig. 65) from St Bees, Cumbria. This extraordinary find was made in 1981 by the archaeologist Dierdre O'Sullivan, in the course of locating the early priory church on the site. The burial had been enclosed in a

65 St Bees man in the process of
undergoing a post mortem, by Dr
Eddy Tapp and his colleagues at West
Cumberland Hospital

lead coffin, actually a single sheet of lead, cut to size and wrapped round the
body, which was then placed inside a wooden box. Upon opening this lead
container, there was revealed a shrouded figure tied up with string, which
was subjected to a full post-mortem examination (fig. 65). This showed the
remarkable degree of preservation, and the presence of certain diseases
including tubercular changes in the lungs and a dental abscess. The man had
also fractured various bones in his jaw in two places during his lifetime.
Although the practice of burial in a lead coffin is well known, from Romano-
British times onwards, no previous bodies in such an excellent state have
actually survived. The video film of the excavation and post-mortem of St
Bees man is extremely gruesome but will undoubtedly remain a splendid
teaching aid on how to deal with well-preserved burials for some time to
come. St Bees man was a nobleman, who died in his early 40s sometime

between 1300 and 1500 AD. His identity is tentatively suggested as Robert de Harrington, who endowed St Bees priory with land and was buried there in 1298. An alternative candidate is Anthony de Lucy who died abroad in 1368 and whose body may have been shipped home in a water-tight coffin, but radio-carbon dates on the skeleton, shroud and coffin may help to elucidate the mystery.

Some of the best-preserved humans survived by accident, like St Bees man, including the famous series of fifth-millennium pre-Dynastic Egyptian burials where bodies had been deposited in shallow graves in the hot sand, often accompanied by simple grave goods. 'Ginger', the gruesome corpse now in a glass case in the British Museum and an irresistible magnet for small boys, is a good example; although his tissues are shrunken and the result grotesque, 'Ginger' is complete almost down to the last hair. Later Egyptian mummification processes can be viewed as attempts to repeat this remarkably good preservation by improving on nature, although the complex rituals frequently had the reverse effect; the ointments, unguents and dehydration procedures employed being considerably less efficient than simply dropping the corpse into hot sand. Another case of man being unable to leave well alone. Egyptian mummification practices were never, in any case, as efficient as those in China (a magnificent example of which is shown in fig. 66), but they improved gradually from first beginnings in early Dynastic times (third millennium) to a peak in the twenty-first Dynasty (c. 1000 BC). They involved variations on the evisceration of certain organs, dehydration of the body using mineral salts, and later stuffing, embalming and oiling before the final wrapping; a process which could take several months. Much of the modern interest in mummification procedures and in the vast amount of information which a well-preserved corpse can give archaeologists, stems from the work of an early pioneer, Sir Max Armand Ruffer, who studied medicine and eventually occupied the chair of bacteriology at Cairo in the late nineteenth century. Many of his publications on a vast range of subjects connected with a lifetime of studying mummies remain of vast importance today, and his work has been carried on by other scientists, notably Professor Rosalie David and her team based at Manchester Museum, with the benefit of full modern scientific aids from x-rays to scanning electron microscopy.

Mummified tissue can provide information about many different aspects of early life, from the blood group of an individual, his diet, diseases and perhaps the cause of his death, to trading practices in Egypt as deduced from resins and salts used in mummification, and changing incidences of pollution and disease. Biochemists are currently trying to isolate the resins used in mummification and identify the areas of conifers from which they came, thus throwing light on Egyptian trade and foreign relations. Chemists at the University of Michigan suggest that levels of lead pollution in ancient Egypt were at least 30 times lower than today – a fact which worries environmental scientists. Studies of mummies can tell us about the longevity of Egyptian

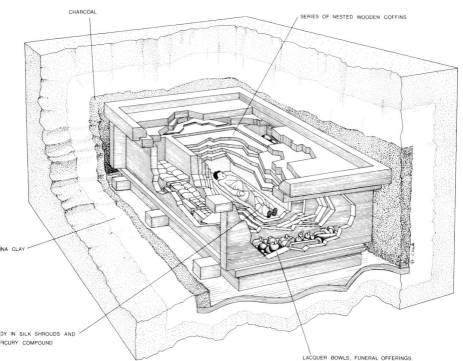

CHARCOAL

SERIES OF NESTED WOODEN COFFINS

NA CLAY

DY IN SILK SHROUDS AND
RCURY COMPOUND

LACQUER BOWLS, FUNERAL OFFERINGS.

66 An extraordinary eighth-century Chinese burial, probably of a queen, who had been shrouded in silks, coated with a mercury compound, and encased in a nest of wooden coffins, each shell being lavishly provided with goods, food and ornaments, before being embedded first in charcoal and then in white china clay. As a result the preservation of the corpse was almost perfect, each joint being still supple. After Hall (1974)

populations, and suggest that the mortality rate did not remain static and that higher social classes had, as one might expect, a greater life expectancy. The average age, at death, of the Ptolemies, who ruled Egypt between 300–31 BC (leaving out those who were assassinated) was a very respectable 64, near the modern European average. But even the pharaohs had their problems, the most universal of which was appalling tooth decay as a result of the high sand content of Egyptian bread. Dental caries was not quite so universal and during the fourth Dynasty seems to have attacked the aristocracy but not the peasants, presumably because they ate different food. Such tombs have, on occasion, produced actual food remains. An intact second Dynasty tomb at Saqquara which had belonged to an important noblewoman produced food offerings laid out on coarse pottery dishes, including a triangular loaf, barley porridge, fish, pigeon stew, a quail, two kidneys, sides of beef, fig stew, various berries, round honey-cakes, cheese and wine. Other tombs produced a wide range of textiles, to say nothing of objects which illustrate not only changing technologies but also the nature and distribution of wealth in society and even elucidate family relationships among the pharaohs. Some of the objects recovered are very fragile, like the fragment of painted linen from a pre-Dynastic tomb at El-Gebelein with an exceptionally fine thread; despite its small size the reconstruction of the fragment (now housed in Turin) was well worth the four years it required. The linen had been painted with a design of ships, each having a double cabin, a bank of rowers and a steersmen in the stern; evidence not only of the type of sea-going ship being used but also of the possibility of maritime contacts with other eastern Mediterranean countries at this crucial period in the development of Egyptian civilization.

For most people, though, it is the actual mummies in Egyptian burial sites which form their most fascinating aspect. However, not all mummies were human; one of the most extraordinary aspects of Egyptian life was their veneration and worship of certain animals believed to be incarnations of the gods, so that we have animal mummies ranging from monkeys to bulls. Cattle and sheep turn up as sand burials as early as late neolithic times (fifth millenium) while in later periods the burial and mummification of sacred animals (over 40 species) became a vital part of Egyptian religious practices. The sacred bulls dedicated to the god Apis were perhaps the largest examples, mummified and buried in huge sarcophagi in the Serapeum at Memphis. The mummification of cows and bullocks *en masse* has enabled experts to study Egyptian cattle-breeding practices and the vast range of animals preserved (antelopes, gazelles, oryx, wild sheep, ibex) illustrates the range of domesticated stock. We find that sheep were not especially important in Egypt since priests were forbidden to wear wool and everyone preferred linen because of the heat. Only the peasants ate mutton. Domestic pets included cats from about 2100 BC (there are 200 mummified examples from Gizeh of two distinct varieties) together with dogs, baboons, ibises, falcons, crocodiles, snakes and various insects. The mummification of certain animals, especially cats (which it was forbidden to kill by law) occurred in enormous numbers. The zoologist Juliet Clutton-Brock notes that the collections of the British Museum (Natural History) include a cat skull which is a lone surviving specimen from a consignment of 19 tons of cat mummies shipped to England after looting the sacred cat cemetery at Bubastis in the beginning of this century, which were destined to be ground up for fertiliser!

The study of complete cemeteries is clearly going to provide information at a different scale from that available from individual burials. Perhaps the most detailed information sources are urban cemeteries, hitherto little studied, since they tend to belong to the historic period and have thus, in the past, received relatively low archaeological priority except in cases of redevelopment threat. Very recent sites are being investigated in America where the growth of interest in urban archaeology is a reflection of heightened public awareness of the importance of studying the recent past. The urban cemetery combines bioarchaeology with forensic anthropology in making an inter-pretation of the physical remains in the graves and then looking, at a larger scale, at what such information could tell us when integrated with historical records. Dental charts, as used today in 'missing persons' cases, may elucidate family relationships; trace-element analysis and x-rays together with historic records can tell us about environment, diet and status. The work of Ivor Noel Hume at the seventeenth-century site of Wolstenholme Tower in Virginia provides an example of this at a micro scale. Martin's Hundred, part of the Wolstenholme site, was the scene of an Indian massacre on March 22 1622, and excavation revealed the skeletons of many of the victims. These included the battered and scalped remains of Richard Kean, a Wolstenholme lieutenant, who was precisely identified.

On a much larger scale there is the late nineteenth-century burial ground at Oakland Cemetery, Atlanta, Georgia, which contained several thousand burials. The Oakland cemetery was one example of a large burial ground near the outskirts of the city to cope with the overflow from crowded urban cemeteries. A similar solution was achieved in Victorian England where many suburban burial grounds are found. Historical records enabled the foundation and expansion of the Oakland cemetery to be precisely charted and in 1976, in response to the earmarking of 2.3ha of the cemetery for potential redevelopment, a study project was set up, correlating historic records, information from elderly locals and, eventually, the results of excavations. Because of the size of the area a sampling strategy was required, which resulted in the cutting of 13 3m-wide trenches. Archaeological evidence produced artefacts from Middle Archaic Period (*c*.4500 BC) to Civil War, as well as nearly 400 grave pits out of an estimated 7,575 in the entire 2.3ha study area – a density of 1 burial per 3 square metres. All sorts of interesting information can be obtained from such a statistically valid sample. Although in this case the historical records were not good enough to identify individuals by name if their graves were unmarked, they could link skeletal remains to funerary rituals and social status. Most of the burials were those of paupers, made in simple pine coffins at the city's expense, although some were more elaborate – fancy coffin fixtures, personal ornaments and grave offerings suggesting higher status. Buttons and buckles from clothes survived but no shoes were found which suggests that the dead were buried without shoes as a result of custom (and economics). The excavators concluded that this segment of the huge cemetery had been mostly concerned with the socially deprived black Atlantans, both from historical records and racial affinities detected from the physical anthropology of the skeletons. Historical records suggest that, apart from disease, the greatest cause of death among nineteenth-century black men in Atlanta was railroad accidents and some evidence of this was found, including a young adult male who had apparently had his feet severed. Height and sex were calculated, where possible, for each burial and this seemed to be roughly correlated with grave size. Trace-element analysis of bone showed that the individuals had had a balanced and varied diet. The interest of the project, apart from its approach, lay in the way that it charted the presence of an element of society which was almost totally absent from the historical records of the period, which mainly deal with the lives of white citizens who rebuilt the city after the Civil War. Their graves, in another part of the cemetery, are often marked by elaborate stone monuments, but this small project produced valuable data about a lesser-known segment of the population, complementing the historical sources.

The above examples illustrate the tremendous range of variation in the quantity and quality of information which archaeologists may obtain from burials. This depends upon a series of factors, including the condition of the burial, state of preservation of the human remains and associated artefacts and the standard of excavation. Some problems seem destined to remain unanswered. For example, why, during much of the British Iron Age, is there no evidence for burial practices although ample evidence for settlement? Many reasons could be advanced; cremation followed by scattering of the ashes, cremation or inhumations with no containers (and thus a smaller chance of survival), or exposure of the dead. People undoubtedly died during this period but we only have evidence of the way they lived, resulting in an incomplete picture of Iron Age society.

The scale at which information about funerary practices may be produced varies with the number of burials; as we have seen, an individual burial may produce data concerning burial rites and the personal characteristics of the corpse which may, indirectly, illuminate some facet of ancient life or palaeoenvironment. However, a collective or multiple burial, especially in the historic period, enables us to use the full range of analytical tools available to archaeologists via physical anthropology, and to find out something about a population, not merely one of its constituent parts. This is not to say that the excavation of a single burial is unjustified – all information about ancient peoples is valuable, it is just that some information is more valuable than others. In the study of burials, as in other branches of archaeology, we are moving away from concentrating in a rather narrow way upon individual items of data and attempting to gain some perspective. We are becoming more critical of our data and realising that in order to obtain first-class results we must have statistically reliable samples. The Oakland cemetery, described above, is an example of this rigorous approach, whereas the burial of Tutankhamun, although fascinating from the point of view of body preservation, burial rites and magnificent grave goods, is only a single (if spectacular) example. Burials are the most obvious focus for ritual activity in any culture and arguably the most emotive branch of archaeology, since we are dealing with the tangible remains of our ancestors (even if they are frequently somewhat fragmentary) and that, after all, is what archaeology is all about.

8
Predictions

It has long been an archaeological truism that distribution maps (such as fig. 2) map the distribution of archaeologists, not sites. One early study showed that in pre-war England almost every archaeological site discovered was within less than 8km of a railway station, and another illustrated an ominously close relationship between site distribution and pubs. It is also possible to plot out the relationship between the catchment areas of various institutions employing archaeologists, such as museums or universities, and site locations or, alternatively, the relationship between the varying research interests of different archaeologists and newly found sites related to those interests. Since archaeological cover of such a large area as England is inevitably going to be uneven, many such distributions are meaningless. Unless the area surveyed has been subjected to a quantitive sampling procedure or a total survey, the distribution of any feature is going to be biased. Close parallels exist between, let us say, the activities of an archaeologist studying the remains of hunter-gatherer communities in a semi-desert area, and the activities of the hunter-gatherers themselves. Fig. 67 shows a map of part of the Central Namib desert, South-West Africa, which the writer has been systematically studying for five years, using two to three month field seasons and visiting the area only during the 'winter' months. Only one main base was established, at the research station at Gobabeb on the River Kuiseb, where the only permanent source of fresh water was to be found. This is the only site where structural remains of this archaeological project would survive, in the form of a whole building complex with indications of craft specialisation (laboratories, vehicle maintenance sheds), some evidence of transport, and ample evidence for diet and drainage. This site is permanently occupied and might be expected to show some evidence of social heirarchy, in the variation in size between the households of the permanent staff, visiting staff and station workmen, as well as activity and recreation areas (a tennis court). The main base is the centre of a nexus of semi-permanent camps, often occupied for one season only, strategically located to study (= exploit) certain archaeological resources. Their location is governed by accessibility (they are unlikely to be located in impenetrable regions of the sand sea) and topography (very abrupt slopes are excluded and the likelihood of occupying low-lying ground such as the river bed is remote).

Each camp of this type would tend to be occupied in stretches of between

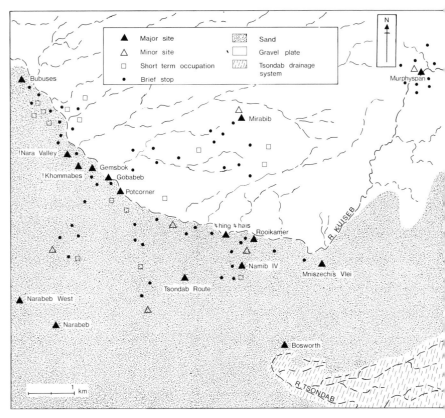

67 The distribution of modern archaeological localities in the Namib (shown here on a scale from brief stops to major sites) makes a curious parallel for the ancient sites. So how will the archaeologists of the future interpret them?

three and seven days at a time (this being the maximum that suppliers of food, water and petrol will last without logistical complications), but the same site may have been reoccupied several times. It should produce evidence of a full range of occupations including tool-making and food preparation, but there will be little structural evidence since the shelters were tents, with the exception of latrines/rubbish pits and the occasional pile of stones used to surround a hearth. Little interaction has taken place with the surrounding environment and archaeological visibility would be low. A third category, temporary camps, have even lower archaeological visibility since they may be occupied just for the course of a day, or as an overnight stop, without the erection of any kind of shelter. The reason for their existence is an archaeological one, to study some particular site, and they are seldom reused. Some will be resource specific (e.g. dumps of water or petrol). The food

68 A site hut on a modern excavation will perform many functions and shelter an interesting variety of people. Would it be possible for future archaeologists to detect these functions?

remains from any of these sites will be exclusively derived from sources outside the area and can provide no clue to local environments; except the few clues from its nature. Thus the almost complete lack of fresh food and preponderance of tins would suggest firstly that the eaters of the food had had some form of transport and had not carried the food themselves, and secondly that some form of heating was involved which left few archaeological traces (a Camping Gaz stove). In this case the nature of the environment at the time of habitation controlled the type of food consumed, and the activities being undertaken controlled the type and density of the site remains. Even so, these temporary camps would be far outnumbered by 'occasional halts' (taking a drink of water, admiring the view, changing a tyre, having a tea-break) which may be archaeologically invisible with the exception of the occasional artefact, but from which no organic material may survive. In this case the main base was supported by six semi-permanent camps, 15 temporary camps and over 60 occasional halts, and in order to stand a chance of reconstructing the full range of activities carried out, examples of all categories of site would have to be examined as proportional random samples of all available sites. In this area an additional complication is provided by the environment which is, south of the River Kuiseb, mobile sand dunes where the archaeological visibility is low. Future archaeologists, endeavouring to reconstruct twentieth-century activities and palaeoenvironments from this type of pattern could very easily come to totally erroneous conclusions.

A further instructive parallel may be drawn taking the excavation site hut, at some hypothetical British excavation (fig. 68), as an example of a human habitat with varied organic remains. Such a structure will be 'occupied', for short periods but on a semi-permanent basis, by varying numbers of people of different social status and occupation. These will include a wide range of artisans (scribes, draughtsmen, cooks, surveyors etc.), workmen, and persons of high social status engaged in non-manual supervisory tasks. The site itself performs a number of different functions at the same time, but is generally occupied only during the hours of daylight and for a restricted period of time, perhaps a few months per year. Such an occupation will inevitably occur in the summer months and there may be annual reoccupation. After the excavation has finished little archaeological evidence of the structure will be preserved since it will probably have been of an impermanent nature (such as a portacabin transported to the site by trailer, or a caravan). In the short term minor environmental impact may be observed – changes in vegetation growth where the hut has stood, the remains of telephone cable connections, a pipe leading water from the mains or filled pits which had served the purpose of latrines/rubbish disposal. Some evidence concerning the varied social status and occupation of the inhabitants could be obtained from the rubbish – cigar butts would tend to indicate high status and the remains of roll-your-own cigarettes, persons of less elevated position. Dietary evidence could be obtained from latrine fills but this would not represent the full range of food available to the site occupants and would be biased by factors such as cost, personal preference, type of food suitable for consumption on site and lack of the full range of cooking facilities. However, the cess and rubbish pits should produce activity-related debris (all the rubbish that accumulates from multifarious activities including drawing, finds conservation, record-keeping, tea-making and food/equipment storage) but it is problematic whether or not a realistic picture of the function and site type could be assembled. Although this is an extreme example, and not one met with in antiquity, it does serve to make the point that it is often extremely difficult to envisage ways by which the full range of activities present on a site can be reconstructed from the archaeological record; not only may the evidence be absent but the archaeologist may not be asking the right questions.

Many specialists have suggested ways by which the problem of perspective may be overcome. It is generally agreed that the questions which are asked of deposits rich in organic matter need to be refined. This point was made succinctly by James Greig in the review article already referred to (p. 109) which examined the kinds of information to be obtained from sewage or cess deposits. Careful problem-orientated excavation and sampling must be the starting point for each enquiry, but the production of simple lists of species is no longer an end in itself; the ecofacts must be made to answer questions about the people. In the case of a cesspit it is relatively easy to identify the residues of food plants, but much more complicated to answer such larger questions as 'Did British diet change over the medieval period and what new plants were introduced?' This requires a different approach. We might be able to say what season of the year most of the plants represented grew in, but is it possible to detect dietary changes over the year, and was this different for households at different points on the social scale? One needs to compare the results obtained from environmental analyses with historical records, integrating works on gardening and cookery with descriptions of the functions of different properties and the evidence (from local historians) about changing patterns of building utilisation. A picture of an early lifestyle can only be built up by taking all these things together. There will always be pieces missing and in many cases the evidence will be uneven, but at least we are now getting some idea of what may be achieved by 'thinking big'.

As we know, archaeology is founded on the simple premise that different types of activity result in different collections of artefacts, ecofacts and structures, which may be revealed by fieldwork and excavation and whose secrets are extracted in the laboratory. The pattern of material, whether organic or inorganic, discarded by any community will serve as a means to evaluate the structure of that community, and its relationship with other communities at different levels of scale and complexity. However, it is obviously necessary to evaluate the archaeological record by quantifying data where possible and endeavouring to find its meaning in real terms. One way of doing this, as we have seen, is by utilising experimental approaches, and another is by ethnoarchaeology, studying contemporary human communities and their behaviour in order to use this data in the evaluation of early social activity. This assumes that all human communities have certain things in common, such as the simple fact that they produce and discard rubbish. If one could quantify the relationship between a modern household and its garbage perhaps such information could be used to interpret ancient rubbish deposits? The vast amount of waste products produced by the average English household in the course of a year has been mentioned (p. 109), and in 1978/9 a team of American archaeologists decided to study household waste in districts of modern Milwaukee (Wisconsin) to see whether family income levels, different socio-economic activities and cultural backgrounds were reflected in the rubbish. The results were to be ploughed back into the evaluation of rather older urban archaeological problems.

The amount of rubbish discarded by a household averaged out at around 10kg per week, although houses in areas where families were small and on low income actually discarded more rubbish than other, more affluent, households. This suggests that income and family size cannot be directly correlated with the quantity of rubbish discarded. Low-income households discarded more packing which was related to high consumption of pre-packaged food and purchase of some things in large numbers of small containers, instead of one large container. This has economic and nutritional implications which are not strictly relevant here, but does suggest that households at different economic levels produce different discard patterns and different types of waste. In earlier societies where socio-economic differences may have been even greater, this factor would doubtless have been accentuated, and one might hope that systematic sampling projects from urban deposits would show not only chronological variations in the type and quantity of waste discarded, but also variations which are related to status as well as to other variables such as the function of a particular building or the state of preservation of its material. The Milwaukee Garbage Project showed that archaeological residues relate to food preferences, fashions, the differing tastes of the occupants of individual houses and problems presented by food storage and shopping. Such variables are going to be equally important in the medieval town but much less so in rural communities whose resource base is more limited and where it is easier to detect the differences between those items of rubbish which represent the debris of meals produced from home-grown produce and those items which must have arrived at the site by trade. The catchment areas of rural and urban households are going to be different, and the quality and quantity of information yielded from an examination of their archaeological remains will be related not only to household status but also to economic limitations.

In its very simplest form we can see, in early agricultural communities, the importance of hunting in providing additional protein sources to supplement the rather precarious resource base provided by agriculture. Even in medieval deposits wild foods are eaten along with domestic ones, but in the present day 'wild' foods (game, truffles, caviar) can often be correlated with high social status. From the time that large-scale trade in food and luxury items began, variations in the food habits of individual households can be attributable to many different causes, with the detection of such matters as individual food preferences often remaining archaeologically invisible since they are submerged within a mass of other data. However, it has become imperative to consider food residues not only from the point of view of range of species present, potential domesticates, presence of plant diseases and importation of exotics, but also to look at the archaeological record from a broader-based socio-economic point of view. All of this rests on a sound infrastructure which can only be provided by good sampling procedures and standardised, systematic ways of looking at bioarchaeological material which permit inter-sample comparison. The basic groundwork has now been done – the technical advances of the 1970s and 1980s make it possible to evaluate the status of individual contexts and have laid the foundation for data banks of bioarchaeological information. Such work has already been started. Following the lead of the Ancient Monuments Laboratory, standard methods are now being employed for reporting on finds of animal bone, using measurement by digital callipers clamped round the bone, which enter information directly into a computer. The controlling programme means that the bone data is always recorded in exactly the same way, making the records of each site inter-compatible. Excavation records are being treated in the same way, with the system developed by the Central Excavation Unit, involving the completion of standard record cards whose data is then fed into the computer, being an increasingly popular method of recording on British sites. Standardisation is the cry of the day – the need to make the records of one site or one project available to other workers in the field, by avoiding the inaccuracies which inevitably ensue when information is merely written down in little notebooks, with no attempt at quantification.

Much work is currently being carried out on the development of computer software for site recording, to encompass the whole range of records from plans, sections, context descriptions and sampled organic deposits, right through from pre-excavation planning to computer-assisted publication.

At the recent excavations on the site of Billingsgate, London, where more than 15,000 separate layers were identified, a network of on-site mini-computers was used for this purpose experimentally, transferring results to a larger model for subsequent analysis. Increased attention is also being paid to ensuring that artefact records from new excavations are compatible with the system being developed for museum collections by the Museums' Documentation Association, which is also working on computerised databases. I have been engaged for the past few years, helped by various assistants, in compiling the database which we have called **KRAS** (Keyworded References to Archaeological Science) which will shortly be available, and will enable anyone working within the field to obtain a rapid idea of what has been published on any particular topic over the last seven years by tapping into the database. These archaeological databases are tricky to construct from the computer point of view, since they need to be extremely flexible and capable of almost infinite extension in any direction to cope with new problems that archaeology is constantly throwing up. However, great strides are being made, not only in the development of software, but also in converting archaeologists to the view that a computer is better adapted to the manipulation and storage of very large numbers of precise facts than their own brains (if these facts are properly entered and programmed)!

One of the most significant developments in recent years, connected with increasing interest in the ways in which archaeological deposits form, has been the sub-discipline of taphonomy: studies which illuminate the conditions under which bones accumulate and provide a background to the interpretation of their ecological significance. Most of the work has been done in Africa, notably on sites related to hominid evolution or the archaeology of early tool-using communities, with the object of sorting out crucial questions like post-depositional disturbance or the distortion of bone assemblages by natural agencies of disturbance. Some of the results have been horrifying. Julie Stein, working on a large shell midden site dating to the Archaic period at Carlston Annis, Kentucky, found that in suitable soils earthworms were capable of mixing material, destroying stratigraphy and contaminating deposits within a very short time, but the results were of extremely low archaeological visibility and would frequently be missed.

In 1955 the French anthropologist Maurice Cavalle published a controversial article called 'The Death of Nature' in which he charted the gradual encroachment of human enclaves within the 'natural' world until the point was reached, around 100 years ago, when the amount of 'nature' which survived was so small that it became a novelty, resulting in the tremendous impact of the great nineteenth-century African explorers' stories, after they had entered the fragments of a world which was impossibly exotic to most people who lived in man-made circumstances. In the twentieth century the 'natural' world has practically disappeared – wild plants survive in hothouses and animals in zoos or game parks which are artificially created 'natural' worlds. It is difficult, perhaps impossible, for twentieth-century people to

69 Experimental archaeology is trendy at the moment, and an invaluable source of information. At the Ancient Farm, Butser, several experiments have been carried out in reconstructing Iron Age houses, complete with storage facilities, using actual excavated examples as the models

imagine what life was like in a world where human impact was insignificant – thus, the further one goes back in time the more difficult it becomes for a modern mind to visualize an ancient situation, or understand how early man lived. Archaeologists and anthropologists have tried to overcome this problem in a number of ways, most notably by the study of extant 'primitive' societies before they finally become incorporated into the modern world, and by the application of such studies to the interpretation of the archaeological record. This is inextricably linked with the field of experimental replication, already mentioned in connection with early agriculture (p. 59) and important on several levels. Any excavated data is necessarily interpreted subjectively because excavation is not an empirical technique. Therefore, one must use all the techniques at one's disposal to ensure that both the excavation and interpretation bear the closest possible relationship to the original truth. Experimental archaeology aims to test out archaeological theories and explanations; by the replication of ancient construction techniques, the way in which artefacts were manufactured, stones moved, crops and animals bred.

This is all most praiseworthy, but in recent years a new element has crept in which should, perhaps, be viewed rather more critically, and this is the attempt made to replicate lifestyles. One of the objectives of the Ancient Farm Project at Butser, in Hampshire, was the reconstruction of different types of prehistoric houses (fig. 69), based on the excavated evidence. This provided all sorts of useful information on, for example, the amount of material necessary to construct such houses, their durability under different weather conditions and the constructional skills (and tools) which would have been required by the original fabricators. The different experiments on the farm, the houses and the crops, attracted immense public attention which resulted in the construction, beginning in 1976, of an Iron Age type farm which would function as a 'living museum' and enable the public to envisage what life would have been like in the Iron Age. Not surprisingly the Ancient Farm has become not only a major tourist attraction but also a valuable teaching aid, although the work spawned a project with less laudable motives. In his 1979 book on the Butser Ancient Farm Project, its director, Peter Reynolds, stated quite categorically that:

> There is here no thought of playing at being Iron Age people. Any attempt to relive the remote past is destined to failure, because the knowledge and experience of previous generations are denied us. To replace modern man into a prehistoric context, given the limitations of our own knowledge, is only to observe how modern people may react both to the conditions and to each other (p. 79).

This is quite in accordance with what has already been said above, yet shortly after the establishment of the Ancient Farm another project was set up (at a secret location in southern England) where a group of volunteers did, for the benefits of the BBC rather than for strictly scientific purposes, just what Reynolds had said should not be done; they attempted, under the constant eye of the television cameras and their own self-criticisms, to establish and run an Iron Age farm from nothing, using and making replicas of original artefacts and, after the first few months, utilising only artefacts which they had made. The result was the highly successful TV series 'Living in the Past' which proved popular for many reasons; viewers' questionnaires suggested that they liked to watch the group struggling so hard against the 'natural' world from the safety of their own firesides, and that it also gave them a real insight into what life must have been like for early man, adding the dimensions of mud, cold and fleas missing in so many of the novels and films made around prehistoric themes. Cynics (mostly archaeologists) said that the experiment was a fake; the women had the advantage of the contraceptive pill, when a child was taken ill modern medicine was invoked, the child was taken to hospital and its family eventually left the project, and at all times the group had the constant reassurance of a TV crew just around the corner. The programmes, though entertaining, were of dubious merit. Reynolds is undoubtedly right, yet the public (who after all provide the finances for archaeological research) clearly approved of the idea. Presumably the answer is to treat such 'experiments' as publicity for archaeological work rather than as serious pieces of scientific research, and such experiments, especially when televised, undoubtedly interest many people in a subject which they would not normally pursue.

The power of the mass media in influencing the way in which people think their ancestors lived is considerable. One has only to consider the impact of magnificent junk films like *Raiders of the Lost Ark* which has provided an image of the 'archaeologist' which will persist for a generation, or the snippets of archaeology which appear in every James Bond film and form the foundation for many other Hollywood epics. This interest is being catered for in a number of different ways. Each year more and more archaeological sites are being opened to the public during excavation, archaeologists having realised (belatedly) that visitors, albeit a nuisance, are also a source of revenue. Prime examples are the recent excavations at Coppergate in York, or Billingsgate in London, both of which made extensive provision for on-site visits. York has taken this one stage further, establishing an underground Viking Centre on the site of the five-year excavation of Coppergate, at a cost of over two and a half million pounds, which displays parts of the Viking city discovered on that site as reconstructed Viking buildings and streets. The centre, which opened in April 1984, enables visitors to be transported back in time via four-seater self-guided cars (rather like dodgems) into the township which has been equipped with the latest audio and visual techniques (including smells). An estimated 500,000 visitors a year are expected, making the centre one of the most popular tourist attractions in Britain, produced solely as a result of the immense interest taken by the public in the Coppergate excavations and what they revealed about Viking life. The Viking Centre will be truly a 'window on the past', not a 'living' museum but an evocation done to the best of the archaeologists' ability to display what it was actually like to live in Viking York. Purists may scoff at the inclusion of 25 life-size Viking figures, but it could be that at York we are seeing one of the most important advances in archaeological public relations ever attempted.

Such raising of the public level of awareness of archaeological issues has had many repercussions. The whole field of 'Public Archaeology' is one in which much ink has been expended recently, over issues related to conservation, funding and legal matters. Questions such as whether or not archaeological sites should be universally opened to the public have been aired as a result of the necessary closure of Lascaux and Stonehenge because of public exposure. The closing of Lascaux has provoked the French government into constructing a £1 million replica made of concrete and plaster near the village of Montignac, complete with copies of the original paintings. The fate of individual objects, always an emotive issue, and, even worse, of human remains has led to a number of test cases recently. The bones from the *Mary Rose* (p. 120) were recently under discussion since the site is claimed as a war grave, and the bodies should therefore receive proper burial. This has now been conceded, although it was agreed that the skeletal biologists working on them should be given as long as reasonably possible to complete a report, and that the bones should remain accessible at some time in the future for scholars to examine, since they are a unique collection. Quite the opposite decision was taken at York, where (reported in the 10.12.81 edition of *The Guardian* newspaper) it was reported that all work had ceased on the bones recovered from the 502 graves in the twelfth- or thirteenth-century Jewish burial ground, and that the 50,000 bones were to be reburied on the cemetery site. This was the result of the intervention of the Chief Rabbi, Sir Immanuel Jakobovits, who considered that the dignity shown to human remains even centuries after their death was more important to human civilization than any scientific inquiries. Few archaeologists would agree with him, but the law surrounding the removal and examination of human skeletal material is complex, although currently in the process of clarification. An ironic postscript has now been provided as archaeologists working on the site begin to doubt whether the cemetery is actually Jewish at all! As we said when considering the question of burials above, the disposal and excavation of human remains is one of the most emotive issues in archaeology and it is hardly surprising that it is an area where detailed procedural guidelines are needed in the future. In answer to this plea the Department of the Environment has just produced one of its 'Advisory Notes' about this matter, but nobody can make any sense of it.

What is needed is a long slow look at the conceptual frameworks within which we are considering the individual projects which together comprise the field of environmental archaeology, realising that the production of an isolated list-of-species from an individual context is severely limited in its general relevance, whatever its intrinsic interest. The information contained in this book shows, very superficially, the ways in which bioarchaeology can be used to give us a picture of the workings of human communities at many different levels, broadly spaced both chronologically and geographically and leading quite different lives. However, these 'windows' on antiquity are not enough, and the archaeologist of the future will, quite rightly, probably be obliged to reassess their importance of our understanding of early lifestyles and balance them against the systematic, if less spectacular, studies which are now being undertaken.

Bibliography

General Reading

Behrensmayer, A.K. (1978) *Fossils in the Making* (Chicago University Press)

Brothwell, D. (1981) *Digging up Bones* (2nd ed. London, British Museum [Nat. Hist.])

Butzer, K.W. (1982) *Archaeology as Human Ecology* (Cambridge University Press)

Clutton-Brock, J. (1981) *Domesticated Animals* (Heinemann/British Museum [Nat. Hist.])

Dickens, R.S. (ed. 1982) *Archaeology of Urban America; the search for pattern and process* (Academic Press)

Dimbleby, G.W. (1978) *Plants and Archaeology* (Paladin)

Fagan, B.M. (ed. 1976) *Avenues to Antiquity* (Scientific American Collected Papers)

Hall, A.R. and Kenward, H.K. (1982) *Environmental Archaeology in the Urban Context* (CBA research report 43)

Manchester, K. (1983) *The Archaeology of Disease* (University of Bradford)

Shackley, M.L. (1981) *Environmental Archaeology* (Allen and Unwin)

Perspectives

Adams, R.E.W., *et al.* (1981) 'Radar Mapping, Archaeology, and Ancient Maya Land-Use', *Science* 213. 1457–1463

Daniel, G. (1981) *A Short History of Archaeology* (Thames and Hudson)

Wilson, D.R. (ed. 1975) *Aerial Reconnaissance for Archaeology* (CBA research report 12)

Hunting

Bailey, G. (ed.) (1983) *Hunter-Gatherer Economy in Prehistory: a European perspective* (Cambridge University Press)

Binford, L. (1981) *Bones; Ancient Men and Modern Myths* (Academic Press)

Brain, C.K. (1981) *The Hunters or the Hunted? An Introduction to African Cave Taphonomy* (Chicago University Press)
Clutton-Brock, J. and Grigson, C. (eds.) (1983) *Animals in Archaeology: 1. Hunters and their Prey* (BAR International Series 163)
Deacon, H.J. (1976) 'Where Hunters Gathered: a study of Holocene Stone Age people in the Eastern Cape' *South African Archaeological Society Monograph* Series no. 1
Grigson, C. and Clutton-Brock, J. (eds.) (1983) *Animals in Archaeology: 2. Shell middens, fishes and birds* (BAR International Series 183)
Shackley, M.L. (1984) 'Palaeolithic archaeology of the Central Namib desert' *Cimbebasia Monograph* Series B.4
Speth, J.D. (1983) *Bison Kills and Bone Counts: decision-making by ancient hunters* (Chicago University Press)

Eating

Davies, R.W. (1971) 'The Roman military diet' *Brittania* 3. 122–142
Bender, B. (1975) *Farming in Prehistory: from hunter-gatherer to food producer* (John Baker)
Glob, P.V. (1971) *The Bog People* (Paladin)
Heiser, C.B. (1973) *Seed to Civilization; the story of man's food* (Freeman)
van der Veen, M. (1983) 'Seeds and 'seed-machines'' *Circaea* 1 (2) 61–2
Williams, D. (1977) 'A consideration of the sub-fossil remains of Vitis vinifera L. as evidence of viticulture in Roman Britain' *Brittania* 8 327–34
Wilson, D.G. (1975) 'Plant foods and poisons from medieval Chester' *Jnl. Chester Arch. Soc.* 58. 55–67

Ailing

Borghegyi, S. (1963) 'Pre-Columbian pottery mushrooms from Meso-America' *American Antiquity* 28. 238–48
Cooke, R.C. (1977) *Fungi, Man and his Environment* (Longmans)
Howe, G.M. (1972) *Man, Environment and Disease in Britain* (Pelican)
Lowy, B. (1972) 'Mushroom symbolism in Maya codices' *Mycologia* 64. 816–21
Wells, C. (1966) *Bones, Bodies and Disease* (Thames and Hudson)

Living

Buckland, P.C. (1976) 'The environmental evidence from the Church Street Roman sewer' *The Archaeology of York* (York Archaeological Trust) 14 (1)
Cunliffe, B.W. (1969) 'Roman Bath' *Res. rep. Soc. of Antiquaries* 24

Greig, J. (1985) 'Garderobes, sewers, cesspits and latrines' *Current Archaeology* 85. 49–52

Mellaart, J. (1967) *A Neolithic Town in Anatolia* (Thames and Hudson)

Thomson, M.W. (1967) *Novgorod the Great* (Evely, Adams and Mackay, London)

Wacher, J.S. (1974) *The Towns of Roman Britain* (Batsford)

Wheeler, M. (1968) *The Indus Civilisation* (Cambridge University Press)

Dying

Ashbee, P. (1970) *The Earthen Long Barrow in Britain* (Dent)

Hall, A.J. (1974) 'A lady from China's past' *National Geographic* 145. (5–6). 661–81

Humphreys, S.C. and King, H. (eds) (1981) *Mortality and Immortality: the anthropology and archaeology of death* (Academic Press)

Leca, A.-P. (1980) *The Cult of the Immortal* (Souvenir Press)

Pearson, K. (1984) 'The Family That Came in From the Cold' *Sunday Times Colour Magazine* (April 29) 29–37 (NB book on same subject to be published in 1985 by the Greenland National Museum in co-operation with C.E. Forlag, Copenhagen, entitled *Qilakitsoq*)

Rudenko, S.I. (1970) *Frozen Tombs of Siberia* (Central Books)

Shackley, M.L. (1983) 'Human burials in hut circles at Sylvia Hill, S.W. Africa/Namibia' *Cimbebasia* 3. (3) 102–6

Moving

Coles, J. (ed.) (1975–80) *Somerset Levels papers 1–7* (Cambridge University Press)

Milne, G. and Hobley, B. (1981) 'Waterfront archaeology in Britain and Northern Europe' *CBA Res. Rep.* 41

Olsen, O. and Crumlin-Pedersen, O. (1978) *Five Viking Ships from Roskilde Fjord* (National Museum, Copenhagen)

Rule, M. (1982) *The Mary Rose: the excavation and raising of Henry VIII's flagship* (Conway Maritime Press)

Wright, E.V. (1976) 'The North Ferriby Boats – a guidebook' *Maritime Monographs and Reports* 23. Greenwich

Predictions

Reynolds, P.J. (1979) *Iron Age Farm; The Butser Experiment* (British Museum Publications)

Stein, J.K. (1983) 'Earthworm activity: a source of potential disturbance of archaeological sediments' *American Antiquity* 48 (2) 277–289

Index